D1621933

Building a New Leadership Ladder

Building a New Leadership Ladder

Transforming Male-Dominated Organizations
to Support Women on the Rise

Carol J. Geffner

The MIT Press

Cambridge, Massachusetts | London, England

The MIT Press would like to thank the anonymous peer reviewers who provided comments on drafts of this book. The generous work of academic experts is essential for establishing the authority and quality of our publications. We acknowledge with gratitude the contributions of these otherwise uncredited readers.

This book was set in ITC Stone Serif Std and ITC Stone Sans Std by New Best-set Typesetters Ltd. Printed and bound in the United States of America.

Library of Congress Cataloging-in-Publication Data

Names: Geffner, Carol J., author.
Title: Building a new leadership ladder : transforming male-dominated
   organizations to support women on the rise / Carol J. Geffner.
Description: Cambridge, Massachusetts : The MIT Press, [2023] | Includes
   bibliographical references and index.
Identifiers: LCCN 2022004531 (print) | LCCN 2022004532 (ebook) |
   ISBN 9780262047388 (hardcover) | ISBN 9780262371551 (epub) |
   ISBN 9780262371568 (pdf)
Subjects: LCSH: Women executives. | Career development. | Sex discrimination
   against women. | Leadership—Psychological aspects. | Organizational change.
Classification: LCC HD6054.3 .G384 2023 (print) | LCC HD6054.3 (ebook) |
   DDC 658.4/09—dc23/eng/20220318
LC record available at https://lccn.loc.gov/2022004531
LC ebook record available at https://lccn.loc.gov/2022004532

10 9 8 7 6 5 4 3 2 1

To Ari,
You are my hope and inspiration for a more humane, just, and compassionate tomorrow.
Shine your bright light upon the world.

Contents

Preface

In 2002, I was flying home after a grueling 24-hour trip to attend a board meeting on the other side of the country. When I arrived at the airport with my colleagues from the C-suite, exhausted and ready for a relaxing trip home, the CEO let me know that there were only eight rather than nine seats remaining in first class. Without hesitating, he suggested I take the economy-class ticket and, without discussion, boarded the plane with my peers—the seven men with whom I shared the C-suite. I eventually boarded the plane with all the other passengers in the economy class. By then, my CEO and colleagues were comfortably tucked away in the first-class cabin. It's worth noting that at that time in the company's history it was mandatory that executives fly first class. For the entire flight, I didn't hear a peep from my teammates. No glass of wine was ever sent back as a gesture of gratitude to thank me for giving up a first-class seat. No one even came back to say hello during a six-hour flight. And when we were deplaning, no one waited to walk with me to pick up my bags before heading home.

In some respects, this scenario is benign. There are certainly worse things than flying economy class. Nevertheless, given the circumstances, I lost out on six hours of informal networking with colleagues. In retrospect, I don't think the incident was intentional, but on the flight and for several weeks after the incident I couldn't help but wonder if it had been meant to send a message to me about my status. To move on, I reminded myself that I had been hired into this C-suite position due to my deep expertise in learning, strategy, and large-scale change. The CEO was confident that my capabilities would be instrumental in helping transform the staid, privately held enterprise into a more agile and efficient contemporary organization. Yet even as I forged collegial and friendly relationships with every one of my colleagues, I was routinely reminded that I was "different." This is why the plane incident was revelatory. It demonstrated a chasm that I would delicately navigate throughout my tenure at the organization. The work was fascinating, and if I could go back in time, I would still jump at the opportunity. Fortunately, I learned at a fairly young age that being a woman in a patriarchal setting was bound to pose unique challenges and that these challenges sometimes included being literally or symbolically pushed to the margins.

Over the course of my 30-year career in business and eventually in higher education, I have often found myself breaking new ground as a woman. Many of my roles have come with sacrifices. I have had to fit into organizational cultures I did not necessarily support, struggled to balance my career aspirations with family commitments, and often put my own personal needs, even my health, on the backburner. I know that I am not alone. Most women who end up in leadership positions make similar sacrifices. For some women, the rise to the top entails even greater challenges and sacrifices. Alongside gender, race and ethnicity continue to deeply shape who is viewed as a potential leader and who is subsequently groomed for such positions. However, to build organizations where the leadership truly reflects the diversity found among the rank and file, we need to do more than call on women and other minorities to "lean in." This brings me to my reason for writing this book.

Since I completed my bachelor's degree and entered the workforce in the late 1970s, I have witnessed myriad changes in the workplace. Women now occupy a wider range of positions across sectors. In some cases, these changes reflect lifted restrictions. In the early 1970s, for example, women could not even pursue leadership roles in the US military or enter the academies where most future military leaders are trained. In other cases, the changes reflect the slow march of progress. In business, women now occupy more top leadership roles and are often not the sole female in the executive tier of the organizations where they work. Perhaps most importantly, what has changed is our awareness of the problem. We now appear to live in a world where everyone seems to be talking about gender, diversity, and leadership, and people are continuously trying to come up with solutions to the many persistent challenges in these areas.

Unfortunately, over the course of my career I have also seen how little organizations have changed. Yes, we now live in a world where you can easily pick up a best-selling book on women's leadership or watch a TED Talk on the subject. Yes, we now live in a world where younger women are more likely to be told they can do whatever they like when they grow up and so arrive in the workforce convinced this is possible. But none of this means the rise to the top is necessarily much easier for women now than it was 50 years ago.

Through my work as a strategy, leadership, and change consultant and executive coach and as the director of the Executive Master of Leadership Program at the University of Southern California, I have the privilege of interacting with hundreds of leaders across sectors each year. The stories I hear—both from women and from male allies—confirm that the leadership gap for women is an unrelenting, structural problem that will not be overcome by simply "leaning in" or rising up. Women still struggle to be identified as potential leaders and are often penalized when they attempt to position themselves for future leadership roles. When women do succeed in obtaining an executive position, it is all too often because they have managed to do what is expected of them as women. That is, women's leadership success seems to rest on the ability to leverage traditionally feminine traits while not being permitted to exhibit too many traditionally masculine traits. This may explain why we have yet to see the rise of a female leader who has the confidence and stubbornness of a Mark Zuckerberg or an ego to match that of Elon Musk.

This book is based on my years of experience working in business and as a consultant and on more than 200 hours of interviews with other women leaders across sectors. The first chapter offers a brief status update on the current state of leadership opportunities for women across sectors. Subsequent chapters investigate specific obstacles for women seeking leadership positions and explore why so many popular solutions not only fail but also in some cases deepen the leadership gap for women. This book also explores practical solutions to help women level up in the workplace. To be clear, I am deeply supportive of calls for women to rise up, assert themselves, and dream big. As addressed in chapter 2, women's self-efficacy remains a critical part of the solution. But for women and men to collectively change the number of women of diverse backgrounds who lead organizations and assume positions in the boardroom, women's individual efforts need to be bolstered by structural change at both an organizational and a societal level. To this end, *Building a New Leadership Ladder* is not simply a call to action for women who want to lead but also a call to action for organizations to begin to seriously rethink how and why they elevate certain potential leaders while overlooking others. As this book makes clear, for organizations to work for rather than against women, we need to dismantle and rebuild the structures, practices, and theories that have long guided how we think about and develop leaders.

No one writes a book alone, and this book is no exception. It is the result of decades of conversations with friends, colleagues, and students. It would be impossible to list all the people whose insights have ultimately shaped this book. I would be remiss not to mention a few people in particular, however.

First, I thank Robert Shelton, president of the Giant Magellan Telescope, and Jennifer Eccles, vice president for development at the Giant Magellan Telescope, without whose support I would not have been able to interview many of the esteemed women who offered their time, insights, and experiences to this project.

I also owe my deepest gratitude to each of the amazing women I interviewed for this book. Their courage and love of their respective crafts are inspiring and have paved the way for other women. These women include (in alphabetical order) Alma Burke, Yasmin Beers, RaShall Brackney, Coco Brown, Mary Sue Coleman, France Cordova, Tiffany Felix, Jennifer Grasso, Heidi Hammel, Stephanie Jarvis, Nannerl Keohane, Fiona Ma, Anni Mu, Laura Mosqueda, Janet Napolitano, Ellen Stofan, Mirtha Villereal-Younger, Hiltrud Werner, Joy White, and Maria Zuber. In addition, I interviewed three women who due to the nature of their positions and sectors asked that they not be identified in this book. I thank them for being courageous enough to share their stories of leadership with me.

I also thank my champion and friend Sam Wolgemuth. A champion earlier in my career, Sam saw my potential before I did and pushed me into uncomfortable terrain. It was his belief in me that launched my journey into executive leadership and taught me invaluable lessons about myself as a woman leader in a patriarchal organization. This book is indirectly indebted to his insights and influence on my career.

I am grateful to Emily Taber at MIT Press, whose guidance and belief in this book helped bring it to life. I thank the reviewers, editors, and team at the MIT Press. I couldn't have crafted my story without their wisdom, expertise, and dedication to excellence.

To my friend Kate Eichhorn, words are insufficient to express my appreciation for all you did to bring my voice forward. This book would not have been possible without you. And to my family and friends, who surround me with love and a belief in my capabilities that fuel my spirit and nurture my heart, I'm grateful for your ongoing support.

1

A Status Update on Women's Leadership

This book was inspired and informed by my conversations with exceptional women leaders. Each of the women interviewed for this book is living proof that women can effectively lead, even in traditionally male-dominated fields. The fact that I had the ability to interview such a diverse range of women leaders also says a great deal about the era in which we are living. Forty years ago, I couldn't have carried out the research I did for this book because at the time there would simply not have been enough women in top leadership roles to complete a significant number of qualitative interviews. But this doesn't mean that any field has yet achieved gender parity on the leadership front, nor does it mean that women leaders don't continue to find themselves working under exceptionally more difficult conditions than men in comparable positions.

As I was writing this book over 2020 and 2021, several of the women leaders I interviewed saw their leadership careers suddenly and devastatingly derailed. The reasons for the derailments varied. One of my research participants, working in a male-dominated sector, was let go after a negative performance review, which was heavily influenced by the leadership of her employees' union. Another was subject to a series of false accusations designed to damage her brand. Ultimately, the situation forced her to turn down a high-profile promotion that would have put her on the national stage. Still another participant, who had been elevated into a leadership role to help clean up an organization after a sexual harassment scandal, was given her walking papers because from the organization's perspective, she had been appointed to clean up a mess but not to lead after the crisis. In a sense, these stories say it all—women are increasingly moving into leadership roles across industries and sectors, but even when they arrive, their experience often remains remarkably different than that of their male colleagues.

This chapter drills down on the numbers and unique conditions that have shaped women's progress on the leadership front since 2000 to explore why women continue to struggle to gain footing in the executive ranks. This chapter also explores several less obvious stories: it showcases the ones obscured by the numbers. Even as more women leaders make headlines, in no sector—not even those where women make up most of the workforce—do women come close to dominating top leadership positions. As discussed in the following pages, for this situation to change eventually, the grit and resilience of just a few exceptional women will not be enough. Broader and sustainable change will occur only through a structural upheaval. That is, even in the second decade of the twenty-first century, we are just getting started.

The Numbers

People like to say that there is power in numbers. This may be true, but sometimes change takes more than a critical mass. For example, although health care has historically been dominated by women, senior leadership positions are still male dominated. Indeed, women make up 80 percent of the health-care workforce but occupy only approximately 20 percent of key leadership roles.[1] The bottom line is that while there may be power in numbers, sometimes the most important factor is not how many women are present but rather the specific roles they occupy in an organization. After all, change can happen from the bottom up, but systemic change rarely happens unless it is championed by leadership at the very top. A survey of sectors and industries reveals that this is where women's progress remains painfully slow. Women's leadership in publicly traded companies stands as a case in point.

In 1970, there was only one woman leading a Fortune 500 company. In fact, by 1970 Katherine Graham had been president of the *Washington Post* since 1963 (her title would later change to chief executive officer, CEO). It was not until 1974 that Graham was finally joined on the list by one other female CEO—Marion O. Sandler of Golden West Financial Corporation. For more than a decade, Graham and Sandler were the only women CEOs. In 1987, one other woman joined the list—Linda Wachner of Warnaco Group Inc.—but when Graham retired in 1992, women again occupied only two top leadership positions on the Fortune 500 list. This started to change in 2000, when the number of women leading Fortune 500 companies, which by then included both industrial and nonindustrial companies, started to slowly climb. Four women CEOs appeared on the Fortune 500 list in 2000. Over the next two years, two more women leaders were added. By 2010, women's representation had jumped to 15 with many more women leading Fortune 1000 companies. And between 2000 and 2020 the number of women leading Fortune 500 companies more than doubled. By 2021, 41 women were listed as CEOs of Fortune 500 companies.[2] Although 41 out of 500 is still a small fraction, after years of stagnant growth something had clearly shifted, but what?

A change in attitude about women's leadership may partially account for the increase in the number of women CEOs of Fortune 500 companies since 2000. A more likely explanation is that over the past two decades some publicly traded companies have finally decided to correct a long-standing catch-22 for potential women executives. For a public company to promote a male or female leader to a CEO position, qualified individuals are typically identified by executive search firms and sometimes by members of the board of directors. Qualified candidates were historically those who had already broken through the glass ceiling into a CEO role or executive-level position with profit-and-loss responsibilities. For women, being so identified has long posed a problem since the pool of qualified female candidates was small, at best. In the 2000s, a growing number of companies, including those on the Fortune 500 list, started to relax the prior-CEO requirements and to consider a broader suite of accomplishments, including prior private-company board service and executive positions. A *Harvard Business Review* article by Catherine H. Tinsley and Kate Purmal suggests that this decision had a profound impact. As Tinsley and Purmal found in comparing the career paths of 100 women CEOs of public companies to a comparable male cohort (notably, their samples were drawn from the largest 3,000 publicly traded companies in the United States), "Prior to becoming a public company CEO: Women were significantly more likely to serve on a corporate Board than men . . . [and] . . . [f]or those recruited from the outside, women were almost twice as likely to be promoted from a non-CEO title as men."[3] In other words, changing but by no means lowering the requirements was needed for women to be considered eligible to lead a publicly traded company and offer them an alternative pathway to the C-suite.

Although women's progress on the leadership front has been scaling up in companies of varying size, many other sectors have witnessed uneven progress. Take, for example, the military. Unlike the corporate sector, where women have often struggled but have not been banned from holding leadership roles, until 1967 women in the United States could not attain the rank of general or flag officer. In 1970, this changed when Anna May Hays and Elizabeth

Paschell Hoisington became the army's first female brigadier generals, but their breakthrough would not immediately open the gates for women. More than 40 years later, only 69 of 976 generals and flag officers serving in the US military were women.[4] Between 2010 and 2020, the number of women holding general and flag officer positions increased only slightly. As of 2020, women occupied anywhere from 8 percent of officer roles in the Marine Corps to 23 percent of officer roles in the Coast Guard.[5] Research suggests that prevailing perceptions about women's leadership potential and previous experience requirements (e.g., an expectation that officers have previous experience serving as an aide) remain ongoing obstacles to women's advancement in the military.

Compared to the military, law enforcement has proven even more resistant to change. As of 2016, just 3 percent of police chiefs were women.[6] And since 2016, these numbers have not risen. Indeed, between 2016 and 2020 many women police chiefs have been forced out or voluntarily left their leadership positions.[7] In many respects, this trend is far from surprising. A study on gender by the National Institute of Justice reported in 2019 that a majority of women in policing consider their profession to be toxic, and many still do not feel valued by peers on the job. Worse yet, solving the gender disparity in law enforcement, especially at the top ranks, faces ongoing challenges. As the author of the study observed, "There is limited empirical research on how to increase the number of women in policing, improve the recruitment of outstanding women, and increase the retention and promotion of exceptional women officers."[8]

Whereas women occupy only 3 percent of police chief positions, the numbers seemingly tell a different story in the world of higher education, where they occupy roughly one-third (or 33 percent) of all executive positions. Moreover, as reported in the *Times Higher Education Supplement* in early 2020, 39 (or 19 percent) of the world's top 200 universities now have a female leader.[9] The growing presence of women leading colleges and universities is not entirely surprising since they have long made up at least half of the higher-education workforce. Yet, as previously noted, a higher proportion of women workers doesn't necessarily translate into a higher proportion of women leaders. As a case in point, we haven't seen the same progress in health care where women have also long made up a majority of the workforce.

What do these numbers tell us about the current landscape for women leaders? Research suggests that as more women assume executive-level positions, the likelihood is greater that other women will aspire to assume these roles moving forward.[10] Behind the good news, however, problems persist, sometimes even where women appear to be making significant gains.

Gendered Leadership Funnels

Imagine being the first woman on the board of a major corporation. You will become a beacon for women waiting in the wings, assuring them through your presence that the door is open. However, the tacit understanding among those already occupying the rest of the seats may be that as the first woman in the boardroom, you should be humbled to occupy a seat at the table. Your experience suggests that as the "new kid" you should listen acutely, speak but not assume you will have a voice, and recognize you might not be viewed as an equal colleague. This account may seem hyperbolic, but it is echoed by countless women and supported by my own research.[11] Moreover, board seats are not the only positions where women often discover they are subject to different expectations than their male counterparts.

In 2019, Korn Ferry, a global executive search and organizational consulting firm, conducted a study on the number of women who hold C-suite positions based on data from the 1,000 largest corporations in the United States. It is encouraging that 25 percent of the top-five critical C-suite positions—CEO, chief financial officer (CFO), chief information officer (CIO), chief marketing officer (CMO), and chief human resources offices (CHRO)—are now occupied by women. Examining the data with a microscopic lens reveals a slightly different story, however. Only 6 percent of CEOs and 12.5 percent of CFOs are women, whereas 55 percent of CHROs are women.[12] As already discussed, the lower number of women CEOs still reflects the fact that there are a limited number of women in the leadership pipeline. By contrast, this explanation does not account for the exceptionally low number of women CFOs. As of 2018, 61 percent of accountants and auditors, 53 percent of financial managers, and 37 percent of financial analysts were women, which suggests women are present but systematically screened out of the leadership pipeline.[13] The question is: Why do women continue to be funneled into some but not all types of leadership positions?

According to Korn Ferry's study, the dominance of women in certain roles, especially people-focused roles such as CHRO positions, may have a simple explanation. As their study concluded, women "bring several competencies to the table, including collaboration, agility, empathy, and an ability to coach and influence that are critical to successfully optimizing the leadership of an organization." This is a positive representation of women and their leadership potential, but it also takes for granted the assumption that women and men are essentially different. Whether one attributes these essential differences to biology (i.e., women are hardwired to be more empathetic and better communicators) or socialization (i.e., women are trained from an early age to be more empathetic and better communicators) is of little consequence. In either case, the message is the same: women are predisposed for certain types of roles, specifically those that require exceptional communication and people skills, even when it comes to leadership. On the flipside, the same binary and biologically based thinking can also be used to conclude that women are less suited to other roles (e.g., CEO or

CFO positions) that are often equated with stereotypical male traits (e.g., logic and decisiveness).

Beyond the troubling assumption that women may simply be better cut out for some leadership roles than others, there is also growing evidence that not all leadership roles are equally valued. As William Scarborough reported in the *Harvard Business Review* in 2018, "Female managers are concentrated in fields that emphasize people-centered caring skills," and the occupations where female managers are concentrated are also "those with the largest gender wage gaps."[14] Notably, the wage gap is not minor. CHROs are routinely the lowest-compensated member of the C-suite, often making less than half of what CEOs and CFOs earn. CHROs also may or may not benefit from annual bonuses.[15] The question is: Are CHRO positions underpaid because women tend to occupy these roles, or do women end up being funneled into CHRO roles because they are underpaid positions (or because men avoid pursuing these positions due to their undercompensation)? It seems likely that in this case a combination of factors may be at play. There are also signs that undoing the pay gap within the C-suite may be easier said than done. As Scarborough observes, "Gender, as a system of stratification, has a sneaky way of reproducing itself. As women enter management, gender seems to operate as an organizing logic so that women end up in caring-centered occupations and men in occupations that focus on the production of goods."[16]

Breaking down the gendered corporate funnel will ultimately rest on moving beyond a biology-is-destiny mindset, but this is likely to be an uphill battle for several reasons. Masculinity is still readily upheld as a leadership trait across sectors for one simple reason—when people think about leaders, they tend to imagine a man, and he is usually a white man. In some cases, however, femininity is also promoted as a potential leadership attribute. Researchers have found that at least in some cases women leaders can successfully influence male-dominated organizational cultures by leveraging traits traditionally viewed as feminine, or what they refer to as "strategic femininity."[17] In a study of women leaders on Wall Street, for example, Melissa Fisher found that many successful women strategically utilized nurturing practices and language considered typically feminine.[18] Although such findings are not necessarily negative, they underscore just how deeply ingrained gender-based assumptions and norms continue to be.

The problem, then, appears to be threefold. First, despite recent gains, men still outnumber women across the C-suite. Second, a disproportionate number of women who do gain C-suite roles end up occupying just a few positions, primarily CHRO positions, and these positions tend to be severely undercompensated when compared to other C-suite positions. Moreover, in nearly all cases these positions are also not ones that will ever lead to CEO roles (i.e., CHRO experience is rarely, if ever, viewed as a stepping-stone to more lucrative C-suite positions). Finally, beyond the gendered corporate funnel, both men and women, even women in leadership positions, often continue to reinforce and normalize traditional gender-based behaviors and traits. This, however, may not be the only reason women appear to be funneled, often early in their careers, either out of the leadership pipeline or into a pipeline that can lead only to less well-compensated leadership positions. On this account, it is useful to turn to higher education—the only sector where women now occupy more than a third of leadership roles.

From the outside, women's relative success in obtaining leadership positions in higher education suggests that in this sector they are not subject to the same gender-based funneling effect found in the private sector. A deeper dive into the data, however, reveals that even in sectors where women appear to be increasingly obtaining executive leadership positions, the leadership pipeline may still be structured by certain gender-based practices and may be especially vulnerable to labor-market changes. Indeed, a disproportionate number of the 30 percent of women who lead higher-education institutions do not run doctoral-granting institutions but rather four-year colleges or community colleges. Unfortunately, with few exceptions, senior leadership roles at the college level carry less prestige and lower compensation packages than similar roles at PhD-granting institutions.[19] There are also troubling indications that despite recent advancements, the future of women leaders in higher education may not be guaranteed. A study by the Brookings Institution in 2019 found that the number of tenured women professors has been in decline since the early 2000s.[20] Because most leadership positions in higher education require a prior role as a tenured professor, future leadership growth for women certainly cannot be taken for granted.

Rise of the Celebrity Woman Leader

Over the past decade, names such as Angela Merkel, Nancy Pelosi, Melinda Gates, Michelle Obama, Hillary Clinton, Mary Barra, Sheryl Sandberg, and Kamala Harris have come to occupy a short-list of celebrity leaders around the globe. On the surface, the rise of these luminaries is encouraging. According to one study published in 2019, women role models can offer an inspiration to other women about what is possible and how to show up in tough male-dominated business situations.[21] But the elevated focus on this rarified group of superstar celebrities does not seem to empower other women or lead to an increase in their representation at the executive level. Here, Sheryl Sandberg's thoughts on women's leadership stand as a useful case study.

In 2012, Sandberg was named one of the top-100 most influential people in the world by *Time* magazine. At the time, she was only 43 and had just been appointed the eighth member and first woman member of Facebook's board of directors. Since her Facebook appointment, Sandberg's influence and celebrity have continued to rise not only due to her corporate position but also thanks to her thought leadership on women's leadership. In many respects, she is a shining role model for women, but her rise and rhetoric on how other women can or should follow suit have also proven controversial.

In her book *Lean In: Women, Work, and the Will to Lead* (2013), Sandberg's thesis is clear: "This book makes a case for leaning in, for being ambitious in any pursuit."[22] For many, Sandberg's message is a call to action for women to rise up and start pursuing their ambitions, whatever form they happen to take. However, it would be wrong to assume the book has necessarily led to the rise of more women leaders. A massive disruption in leadership may not be what Sandberg has imagined. She has said herself, "The shift to a more equal world will happen person by person." This approach has left some women wondering who is really served by Sandberg's call to "lean in." After all, if you're a woman attempting to ascend the ranks of a male-dominated organization—one where you may even be regularly dismissed or routinely excluded from networking opportunities—how far do you need to "lean in" for the organization to make room for you? And if the organization does not make room for you, is it your fault as an individual? What role does the organization play in creating the right context in which women can rise?

Sandberg's book has certainly sold many copies (in the year following its release, it sold 4.2 million copies worldwide), but it has also garnered a fair amount of harsh criticism.[23] Not only does Sandberg seem more interested in empowering one person at a time than in a feminist uprising, but she also appears deeply invested in the power of strategic femininity. In her words, "A woman needs to combine niceness with insistence." Although she admits that it may be a paradox to advise women to change the world "by adhering to its biased rules and expectations," she consistently suggests that even if this is an imperfect solution, women should embrace the message because it will lead to desirable outcomes.[24] It is just such advice that led one early critic, the *Guardian* columnist Zoe Williams, to conclude that *Lean In* "is not a book about how women can become more equal" but rather a book about how "women can become more like Sheryl Sandberg."[25] Of course, not everyone can become Sheryl Sandberg or even desires to do so.

In an essay titled "Dig Deep: Beyond Lean In," the feminist critical race studies scholar bell hooks draws attention to Sandberg's unchecked assumptions about race privilege. As hooks notes, "Her vision of individual women leaning in to the corporate table does not include any clear statement of which group of women she is speaking to and about, and the 'lean in' woman is never given a racial identity. If Sandberg has acknowledged that she was primarily addressing privileged white women like herself (a small group working at the top of the corporate hierarchy), then she would not have portrayed herself as sharing a message, indeed a life message, for *all* women."[26] Many other women, including other women of color, have launched similar critiques of Sandberg's call to action.

When Michelle Obama was asked about Sandberg's book at a launch for her own memoir, *Becoming* (2018), she replied without mincing words, "It's not always enough to lean in, because that s**t doesn't work all the time."[27] Although Obama was quick to apologize for her vulgar use of language, she did not retract her critique of Sandberg. Like hooks's assessment, Obama's message suggests that while leaning in may be possible for some women, for many others, including those whose class, location, race, sexual orientation, ethnicity, or even name make the rise to the top even more difficult, leaning in may not be enough. Despite Obama's sharp critique of Sandberg's approach to promoting women's leadership, Obama and Sandberg do share at least one thing in common—both are part of a new generation of celebrity women leaders. But this again raises an obvious question: Why are individual women leaders increasingly gaining celebrity status, and what is the function of these celebrated figures?

In 2015, along with Sandberg and Obama, another celebrity woman leader was making headlines: Elizabeth Holmes. At the time, Holmes, the founder and CEO of the now defunct health-care diagnostics company Theranos, had every reason to be garnering attention. At 31, she was the world's youngest female billionaire. For this reason, it is not surprising that the media was quick to start holding her up as a role model for a new generation. An article in *Inc.* reported in 2015 that Holmes—who had gained a reputation for being aloof—had started to leave the lab to offer motivational speeches to groups of girls. Yet the same article suggested that Holmes may not have been fully aware of the fact that she was a pioneer. In her own words, "It was a long time after I started this company that I realized that there had not been a sole female founder-CEO of a multibillion-dollar health care or technology company. . . . I didn't believe it. I still don't believe it."[28] Whether Holmes was intentionally breaking the glass ceiling, in 2015 everyone appeared to be lauding her ability to do so. When *Time* magazine added her to its 100 Most Influential People list in December 2015, Henry A. Kissinger, who had met Holmes earlier in her career, described the young leader as "striking, somewhat ethereal, iron-willed" and observed, "Elizabeth is in the process of turning an undergraduate's vision into a global reality. That she combines fierce and single-minded dedication with great charm makes her a formidable advocate." Yet there are indications that Kissinger may have already known something that most people did not yet know about Holmes's company. As he further observed, "Others will judge the technical aspects of Theranos, but the social implications are vast."[29]

In the end, the "technical aspects" of Theranos would indeed be judged. A *Wall Street Journal* article by John Carreyrou would reveal in 2015 that Holmes's multibillion-dollar company wasn't based on much science at all.[30] Revelations from the article, which would eventually also lead to a book and documentary, found that Holmes had audaciously raised millions of dollars for a company that had no new product or service to offer. Although Holmes's leadership was by all accounts built on a lie, the media attention given to her between 2014 to 2017 is still relevant to this discussion. At the very least, it points to the strong need for more women leaders, perhaps especially younger women leaders in Silicon Valley. This was certainly the narrative that a feature in *Fortune* sought to tell. As the reporter Michal Lev-Ram observed, Holmes "is used to being the lone woman in the room. She was the only female chemical engineering student in her undergraduate class at Stanford University and is the only female CEO in the so-called 'Decacorn Club' (start-ups with valuations of $10 billion or more). She is even the lone woman at her very own Board meetings."[31]

The image of a young woman leading a successful start-up in a sea of men was compelling for women, but Holmes's rising star was not just the result of being held up as a role model by other women. By 2015, just as Holmes started to land on the cover of nearly every major business magazine in the United States, there was a growing recognition that Silicon Valley's startup culture may be innovative but not necessarily progressive. Indeed, by 2015 Silicon Valley was increasingly coming to be represented as an old boys' club that had simply been staffed with new boys. In many respects, Holmes was the perfect antidote—young, female, and bearing uncanny similarities to Steve Jobs (whether a conscious choice or not, Holmes even dressed like Jobs). She seemed to offer living proof that a young woman could found a company in Silicon Valley, successfully persuade venture capitalists to fund it (even though women founders generally receive less than 3 percent of venture-capital funding), and lead it on her own, even without the support of any women on her own board.[32] Thus, while Holmes's decline had nothing to do with gender (her lack of integrity was her downfall), her rise—and specifically the celebrity status she garnered along the way—seemed to have had a lot to do with gender. What is striking about Holmes's story is that even as she claimed to be virtually oblivious to the fact that gender may hold women back in Silicon Valley, other women were beginning to speak up about the region's exceptionally hard glass ceiling for women and about the toxic culture that had come to define the region's corporate culture.

When neither the Jacket nor the Culture Fits

Beyond the women leaders who have dominated the headlines in the twenty-first century, life in many organizations, including those in traditionally male-dominated fields, continues to look much like it did in the mid–twentieth century. With even more women on the ground, the culture of many organizations still sends an oftentimes subtle message that opportunities for women are limited. But, as suggested, it isn't simply in established organizations with deeply ingrained cultures where this is the case. Many new tech companies, including those established since 2000, have quickly come to replicate cultures that make advancement for ambitious and talented young women difficult, if not impossible. Uber stands as a case in point.

In 2017, Susan Fowler—now a full-time writer but at the time a recently resigned engineer at Uber—published a now infamous blog post, "Reflecting on One Very, Very Strange Year at Uber."[33] In her post, Fowler described how Uber's toxic culture had in just two years led to a mass exodus of women engineers. When Fowler arrived in 2015, she joined an engineering team comprising 25 percent women. By the time she left two years later, women made up just 6 percent of the company's engineers. What was striking about Fowler's account of Uber's culture was that the exclusion of women seemed to permeate every relationship and practice. In fact, in her post Fowler recounted not only overt incidents of sexual harassment (e.g., being repeatedly sexually propositioned by a manager) but also more subtle and insidious incidents, including the so-called jacket incident.

As Fowler recounted, shortly after her arrival at Uber the company decided to order leather jackets for all of its engineers. Everyone tried on a jacket for size and placed an order. Months later, all the women received an email saying they would not get a leather jacket after all. The company, which reported $6.5 billion in revenue in 2016, claimed that it could not afford to order leather jackets for the women because with so few women left on the team it would not be able to take advantage of a bulk discount in ordering the sizes they needed.[34] In a strange twist, when Uber's women complained, they were told the decision was ultimately about supporting equality. After all, how would they feel walking around wearing a leather jacket that cost significantly more than the jackets being worn by their male colleagues?

While the jacket incident at Uber may sound minor, it is by no means insignificant. Matching jackets are a simple way to communicate a unified sense of belonging—a symbolic bonding of sorts. If the jackets are about symbolic bonding, the underlying message to the women at Uber was clear—they were different, on the periphery, and would quite literally never fit in.

The culture of Uber may have been exceptionally toxic for women, but it is by no means an outlier. In Silicon Valley, employees may be permitted to dress like every day is casual Friday, but behind the casual clothes, beanbag chairs, and snack stations, the culture of many of these new companies doesn't look much different than the culture of organizations in the 1950s.

Shortly after the debacle at Uber in 2017, a team of Stanford University researchers surveyed more than 200 women working primarily at Bay Area and Silicon Valley tech firms. Among the women surveyed, 25 percent held chief experience officer (CXO) roles, 11 percent identified as founders, and 11 percent worked in venture capital. There were also women with executive positions at Apple, Google, and dozens of other established tech companies and venture-capital firms. The findings, eventually published in the appropriately titled report "An Elephant in the Valley," revealed an established culture of sexism across the region's tech companies and venture-capital firms. According to the study, 66 percent of the women surveyed had felt excluded from key social/networking opportunities due to their gender, 59 percent felt they had not been afforded the same opportunities as their male counterparts, and 90 percent had witnessed sexist behavior at company offsites and other industry conferences.[35]

The revelations about the toxic culture for women in Silicon Valley came as a shock to some people and a disappointment to others. Worse yet, some studies suggested that Silicon Valley start-ups may be even more toxic than start-ups in other regions. One study published in 2017 found that women were far less likely to lead venture-backed startups in Silicon Valley than in nearly any other major US market, including New York City.[36] But this raises a critical question: Does culture really matter? With enough grit and stamina, can't women rise despite the odds? Although there are certainly exceptions to the rule—indeed, this book highlights dozens of women who have risen to the top despite working in deeply sexist cultures—culture does matter.

To understand the powerful effects of culture on leadership, put yourself in the shoes of a woman in law enforcement. Through tenacity, physical proficiency, courage, and resilience, you make it through the rough-and-tumble training period and enter a profession defined by patriarchal traditions. The first few years you gradually figure out the unspoken rules of the game and hope that hard work and "getting along" will ultimately lead to promotion opportunities. Yet all that still isn't enough. As one police chief interviewed for this book (who felt she needed to remain anonymous) explained, early in her career her supervisor openly said, "You just don't get how things work around here. What do you think you are, a hero?" The comment, she explained, seemed to have two aims—to remind her of her outsider status and to let her know that she would never be part of the boys' club that held power in the organization. Unfortunately, this comment is not unique. It and the many others like it reflect a culture in which women must depersonalize outright bullying and sexist behavior to survive and eventually rise through the ranks.

To be fair, women and men alike struggle when there is a poor cultural fit in the workplace. In the case of women in male-dominated sectors, however, the stakes of these cultural mismatches may be greater. Mariela V. Campuzano, who studies the organizational culture of health-care organizations, observes, "In male-dominated organizational cultures where men are the majority, socially learned underlying assumptions are reinforced over time. Because leadership is more easily welcomed when it stems from familiar traditions within a culture, promotion to leadership in dominant industries and organizations typically benefits employees who embrace a historical workplace culture versus deviations from it."[37] According to Campuzano, when women do manage to break through in these organizations, the breakthrough is also most often viewed as a "variation." As a result, they still face a notable burden—the need to comply with and even uphold socially learned workplace values and norms, including those that have made and continue to make their own success tenuous. This brings us back to Uber's "jacket incident."

Workplace culture certainly cannot be reduced to symbols such as a company-logo jacket. Yet as the organization psychologist Edgar Schein suggests, "artifacts," alongside values and underlying assumptions, are powerful aspects of any organizational culture.[38] A company jacket, then, is always more than an accessory—it is a highly visible manifestation of one's workplace culture and whether one fits into that culture. What if the jacket does not fit, and no one is willing to order a jacket that does fit? What if the jacket comes in only one or two sizes, and neither is designed to fit the average woman? In such cases, women have two choices: they can either not wear the "uniform" or wear an ill-fitting jacket made for an average-size biological male. Either way, the choice leads to a variation—you might be on the team, but you will stand out whatever choice you make. Said differently, when the culture does not fit, women may still rise to the top, but the burden is on them to comply with and even reproduce a culture that will never quite fit. This is precisely what *Building a New Leadership Ladder* seeks to explore—how women's prospects to lead, especially in male-dominated professions and sectors, must be understood as an organizational rather than individual project.

Looking Ahead

During the more than 200 hours of interviews carried out for this book, one thing became clear to me—women who rise to the top of their professions still face obstacles that their male counterparts do not. From overtly toxic workplace cultures to gender-based expectations about one's potential, in the twenty-first century the leadership ladder for women remains rife with obstacles. For women of color, that landscape is frequently even more hazardous because they must grapple with both gender- and race-based forms of discrimination and may find even fewer role models at the top.

As much as *Building a New Leadership Ladder* is attentive to women's past struggles, its focus is first and foremost on the future. Specifically, this book is concerned with how individual women's ability to effectively lead, although partially rooted in individual will and mindset, is just as contingent on building workplace cultures that support women's rise to the top. Said differently, whatever one might believe about the power of women's grit or personal drive, which are important leadership qualities, bringing about a sustainable change across an entire industry or sector is not something any woman can do on her own. As explored in chapter 2, a woman's individual psychology is essential when it comes leadership, but even the most intelligent, gritty, and focused women are frequently no match for a hostile organizational culture, especially one that has historically been designed, intentionally or unintentionally, to diminish, derail, and destabilize them. That is why *Building a New Leadership Ladder* is not just a book for women leaders and women who aspire to lead. It is a call to action for anyone invested in creating structures, practices, and mindsets designed to promote equitable leadership.

2

Mindset versus Organizational Culture

Since 2000, books that purport to offer advice to women on how to rise up the ranks of organizations or to found and lead their own businesses have become increasingly popular. Straddling business, self-help, and leadership theory, these books—which include Sheryl Sandberg's *Lean In*, Brené Brown's *Dare to Lead* (2018), Sophie Amoruso's *#Girlboss* (2014), and other best sellers—seem to have at least one thing in common: they place the onus mostly or entirely on the individual woman to break through the glass ceiling, implying that change is ultimately an inside-out process. In essence, these books' underlying message is that if women change (e.g., become more confident, gritty, tenacious, etc.), they can force organizations and even entire sectors to make room for them to rise up and take control.

Admittedly, I appreciate the spirit of these books. For all their faults, they are bold calls to action, and their impressive sales figures stand as a testament to just how many women are eager to embrace these calls to action. But is what they accentuate really how organizational change works, especially for women who have historically faced both gender and racial discrimination in the workplace? How, then, do we explain the fact that Black women are more likely to actively pursue leadership roles than nearly any other demographic and yet are also more likely to be overlooked for leadership roles?[1] If one's sense of purpose and intentional pursuit of leadership positions were all it took to change the C-suite, we would be already living in a world where board rooms are dominated by Black women leaders. This was a point raised in my interview with Tiffany Felix, the senior vice president of environmental health and safety at ViacomCBS.

During our interview, Felix told me about an experience she had early on in her career. At the time, she was about to leave a large media company for which she had worked for several years because it had become apparent that it offered no further room for advancement. In a conversation with a senior executive who claimed to be committed to diversity, she asked him why there were so few women and no women of color at the C-suite level. In response, he admitted, "We tend to self-select." As Felix told me, "I was glad he said that. It was an honest answer. Of course, he could be self-selective— choose to work with people who looked exactly like him—because if you walk into a board room and it's full of white men, no one is going to question your tendency to work with people who resemble you. If I started to do this, and someone walked in and discovered everyone on my team was a Black woman, there would be a lot of questions." Felix's account is significant. It highlights, among other things, the fact that no matter how ambitious a woman may be, if an organization is unwilling to change, it may still be impossible for her to keep growing on the job and eventually assume a leadership position. In this case, Felix—who has always had a strong sense of purpose and clear line of sight on both her short-term and long-term leadership goals—decided to pursue a horizontal move rather than stay and stagnate in her current organization. As this chapter demonstrates, her experience isn't unique.

One can possess a phenomenal tool kit of leadership attributes and yet, depending on the organization, still hit a glass ceiling or, worse yet, a brick wall. To this end, this chapter drills down on seven leadership attributes and considers what these qualities or attributes mean when adopted by or applied to women. Although there is ample reason to conclude that cultivating known leadership attributes such as curiosity, mastery, purpose, self-awareness, courage, resilience, and optimism is important, ingrained practices and cultural norms in the workplace often continue to erode and undermine women's efforts to leverage these qualities. This chapter begins by examining two of the most frequently discussed and lauded leadership qualities for men and women—curiosity and mastery.

Women Leaders as Experts—Curiosity and Mastery

A quick survey of research and advice literature on leadership reveals that curiosity and mastery are among the most frequently lauded leadership qualities. These attributes were also themes that emerged in my own interviews with women leaders, especially those working in science, technology, engineering, and math (STEM) fields.

Consider, for example, Mary Sue Coleman—a chemist by training, the former president of the Association of American Universities, the thirteenth president of the University of Michigan, and the eighteenth president of the University of Iowa. Coleman spoke at length about the insatiable curiosity that has driven her forward throughout her career. "Every time I took a new position," she said, "I just told myself that I could do it. I knew a few of the jobs were an enormous leap, but each time I learned to sharpen my attention and observational skills just a bit more and dug in to learn everything I could." Ellen Stofan, under secretary for science and research at the Smithsonian and former NASA chief scientist, likewise credited her analytic acumen as a core attribute in unpacking the puzzle pieces of any problem. As she observed, her scientific training had prepared her to approach challenges with an investigative mindset, which was essential not only in the lab early on but also in navigating the traditionally male-dominated organizations in which she eventually came to assume leadership roles.

In many respects, these interviews simply reinforced what I, as an organizational behavior and learning expert, already knew to be true—that curiosity is central to building cultures of innovation, learning, and performance. However, my interviews also revealed that curiosity also seems to play a significant role in helping women leaders analyze and address the complex and often troublesome scenarios that emerge over the course of a professional career. This certainly held true for Joy White, executive director of the Air Force Space and Missile Systems Center.

White told me that curiosity has long been at the core of her professional success. Because she has always been interested in discovering what she could learn from a new position, she has been willing to take on new positions, whether they represented a move up the ranks or an undeserved move downrank. As she emphasized in our conversation, at times she even accepted jobs no one else wanted. When I asked why, she explained, "Accepting positions no one else was willing to take on was one of the ways I kept learning and growing professionally."

Although taking on positions that may feel below one's level of expertise and experience or that are unwanted by others may seem counterintuitive, there is evidence that White's impulse to do so was correct. Here, the work of Francesca Gino, a behavioral scientist and the Tandon Family Professor of Business Administration at Harvard Business School, stands as a case in point. In a controlled setting, Gino asked groups of five to six executives to complete a task that heightened their curiosity and then asked them to engage in a simulation that tracked their performance. Gino and her colleagues found that the groups whose curiosity had been heightened outperformed the control groups, who had received a prompt to trigger

reflection but not raise curiosity, "because they shared information more openly and listened more carefully."[2] Other studies have
found that curiosity in turn supports an array of broader leadership
traits, including solid decision making,[3] creativity, and innovation.[4]
As it turns out, though, curiosity also seems to support one's ability to endure and even make the most of undesirable positions and
situations on the job and to keep growing in ways that hold the
potential to cultivate one's leadership capacities over time.

Yet even though there is compelling reason to believe that curiosity generally serves women well in their pursuit of leadership roles
even when they face major setbacks, when their curiosity leads to
mastery, as it often does, the effects may or may not be entirely
positive.

On the one hand, the women I interviewed for this book unani-
mously underscored the importance of always being the best and
meeting the very highest performance standards. Most emphasized
that good is never good enough. As aptly stated by one law enforcement leader (who asked that her name not be used in this book)
who had been passed over for promotions on numerous occasions,
often by men with far less experience, "I eventually made it tough
for them to say no. I wanted them to have to say, 'Why not her?,'
because I had reached a point where I was clearly the most qualified
individual available to step up."

Among all my interviews, however, two women's accounts stand
out as particularly poignant. The first account is from a woman
who is a former special weapons and tactics (SWAT) officer—one
of the toughest positions in law enforcement. She credited always
striving to exceed expectations as an essential ingredient in gaining respect from her male colleagues. As she told me, "There is
always extra scrutiny." On one occasion when she was on patrol,
she overheard a few male colleagues on the police radio making fun
of her and her female partner. As one of them said, "Let's watch her.
She and her female partner are going to need our help." This was

one of the more benign encounters she had on the job, but it was by no means exceptional. Women in traditionally male-dominated settings generally know that they have to outperform their male colleagues at all times just to be viewed as capable. But this general rule doesn't apply just to women in male-dominated fields such as STEM, law enforcement, and the military. Fiona Ma, California's state treasurer, told me that it doesn't matter how far she rises in her career; as a woman and visible minority, she still feels an impetus to do additional homework, master every subject inside and out, and make every effort possible to understand stakeholders' motivations. She credited her commitment to mastery as the primary reason her recommendations and points of view have been heard even when she is promoting an unpopular position on a matter of public interest.

Mastery, like curiosity, was cited as a central leadership quality in my interviews for this book, but there is evidence that it may serve women somewhat differently than it serves men. For those who also suffer from what some people may label "imposter syndrome" (a syndrome most often experienced by highly successful individuals who doubt their abilities and feel like a fraud), mastery is frequently pursued out of a desire to ensure one is never "found out" by their peers. Here, internal scripts (e.g., a feeling that they don't deserve to occupy a specific position) are often at work.[5] However, for women, mastery also seems to raise other challenges rarely experienced by men. For example, at least in STEM fields women who communicate their research findings in both academic and nonacademic settings are more likely to be negatively characterized by male and female colleagues alike.[6] A study published in 2018 suggests that the bias against women's mastery negatively impacts women not only as their careers advance but even at the entry level. For her study, Natasha Quadlin conducted an audit by submitting 2,106 job applications in which she experimentally manipulated the grade-point average (GPA), gender, and college major of applicants. Her findings were somewhat alarming. She discovered that high-achieving men (those with high GPAs) were called back significantly more often than high-achieving women—on average, twice as likely. In STEM fields, the call-back rate for men was much greater—they were called back three times more often than women. Quadlin concluded that whereas men with a variety of GPAs land job interviews, women seem to benefit from moderate achievement but not from high achievement.[7] Such findings suggest that although mastery is needed for women to excel, possessing it is not without consequence, creating a rather obvious catch-22 for women, especially those in traditional STEM fields.

When Women Find Their "True North"—Purpose and Self-Awareness

A PwC study in 2016 found that 79 percent of business leaders believe that purpose matters when it comes to business success.[8] For women leaders, however, purpose seems to hold specific import, but, once again, its effects both support and undermine women's efforts to rise to the top ranks.

A study by Marlene G. Fine in 2009 found that women leaders seem especially inclined to believe that leadership is linked to service. As she discovered, for many women leaders, "without service, leadership has no purpose" and purpose is often the key reason they assume leadership roles.[9] Likewise, a study by Herminia Ibarra, Robin Ely, and Deborah Kolb in 2013 found that an effective way to support women on their path to leadership is to "anchor women's development efforts in a sense of leadership purpose."[10] A study by three Columbia Business School researchers in 2020 further found that purpose may be an especially important career driver early on, impacting everything from the type of courses one opts to take in graduate school to the kind of internships one chooses to pursue.

The same study concluded that purpose may be so important to women that it even comes at a cost. Because women appear more willing than men to make sacrifices (e.g., settle for lower compensation) to pursue positions or work in industries that offer greater purpose (e.g., the nonprofit sector), they often end up making less over time and selecting themselves out of sectors with the most prestigious leadership roles.[11]

Although purpose is certainly important to men and women alike, in my interviews for this book I found that purpose not only was essential to every woman leader I encountered but also seemed to serve a different function for women than it does for most men. Here, it's useful to return to the work of the leadership expert Bill George, who famously called on leaders to "find their true north"— identify their central purpose and core beliefs—the assumption being that their "true north" will become a guidepost as they pursue their higher calling. For most of the women I interviewed, however, purpose seemed to be just as likely to serve as a guidepost under very different conditions—that is, when they were being derailed or thrown off course in the face of aggressions or microaggressions in the workplace.

One of my participants, a former university president who continues to teach, told me the primary reason she pursued an administrative leadership role in the first place was to build the capabilities of the next generation of women leaders. When she was suddenly let go from a high-profile university leadership position without explanation, her "true north" helped her recover from the setback and humbly step back into a department-level teaching role.

A related concept—self-awareness—operates in a similar manner: it seems to be critical for women and men alike who wish to pursue leadership roles, but women also seem to require self-awareness to stay on course when the path ahead is strewn with obstacles.

In 2013, Tasha Eurich embarked on a study of self-awareness that would include 5,000 participants. According to Eurich, self-awareness happens both internally and externally. Internal self-awareness impacts how we see our values, passions, aspirations, and effect on others. External self-awareness impacts how we view others and their values, passions, aspirations, and effect on others.[12] It is no surprise, then, that self-awareness is also equated with a wide range of leadership traits. When we are self-aware, we're more confident, more creative, more honest, better at making decisions, and better able to cultivate stronger relationships. As a result, we're also more effective leaders who have happier employees and more profitable companies.[13] For women leaders, however, self-awareness is essential for another reason—not unlike purpose, it also seems to be critical to dealing with microaggressions in the workplace.

The term *microaggressions* has been in use since the early 1970s, but the modern definition of it is usually credited to Derald Wing Sue, a professor of counseling psychology at Columbia University who has written extensively about the subject. Wing Sue defines microaggressions as "everyday verbal, nonverbal, and environmental slights, snubs, or insults, whether intentional or unintentional, which communicate hostile, derogatory, or negative messages" that "target persons based solely upon their marginalized group membership." Often discussed in relation to racism, microaggressions can also target women, members of the LGBTQ community, differently abled individuals, and other minorities.[14] Because microaggressions, unlike overt forms of discrimination, tend to wear people down over time—one small comment or action at a time—they can be challenging to identify or call out, especially in the workplace.

Consider the experience a colleague of mine had when she attended a graduation ceremony at the liberal arts college where she teaches literature. At the time, she was 41, had a PhD, and had published four books. While standing in line waiting to walk onto the stage with the other faculty, a male colleague from another department who was in his late forties turned to her and said, "Congratulations!" When she asked why she was being congratulated, he said, "For completing your BA." My colleague was stunned. She was wearing the same graduation regalia as her male colleague and standing in line with other faculty waiting to go on stage, so how could she be mistaken for an undergraduate? When she pointed this out to her male colleague, he laughed and said, somewhat predictably, that this was a huge compliment to her since she still looked 22. Most people wouldn't consider this incident the stuff of a Title IX complaint, and yet it is just such incidents that often over time cause the most damage to women and other minorities in the workplace. Single incidents may seem minor. When they repeatedly happen, though, they can and often do wear down women, slowly eroding their sense of purpose, confidence, and self-efficacy.

Like purpose, self-awareness *can't* prevent one from experiencing microaggressions in the workplace, but it can help one stay on course, even when being derailed. So, does an individual woman's sense of purpose or self-awareness matter when it comes to leadership? The answer is yes, but not for the same reasons these attributes seem to serve most men in the workplace. This distinction doesn't make these qualities any less important for women—in fact, having a clear sense of purpose and being self-aware may be even more essential for women leaders. What's clear is that these attributes may or may not lead women to the top. After all, if you're always dodging bullets, reaching a pinnacle is certainly not a given.

The Long Journey to the Top—Courage, Resilience, and Optimism

The final set of leadership qualities I want to consider in this chapter are courage, resilience, and optimism. These three qualities aren't just frequently discussed in leadership literature but are also especially important themes in the many trade books now on the market that target aspiring women leaders. Again, although I happen to believe that courage, resilience, and optimism are important leadership attributes, the question remains, What are we suggesting when we tell women that these attributes matter more than anything else?

Take, for example, courage. Courage is a key theme of both Sandberg's *Lean In* and Brown's *Dare to Lead*, and many women apparently take this theme away from reading these books. In fact, on retail sites such as Etsy, you can even purchase coffee mugs and T-shirts emblazoned with Brené Brown's declaration "courage over comfort" and wall art featuring Sheryl Sandberg's mantra, "Ask yourself, what would I do if I weren't afraid? Then go do it." But what does courage actually mean for women who aspire to lead?

First, imagine being the newly appointed president of a large institution, attending the first welcoming cocktail party sponsored by the institution's board, and then learning after the party that a board member had used the occasion to corner your spouse and tell him that he didn't think you were up to the job. The leader who shared this story (who did not want her name used in relation to this specific incident) told me that it took tremendous courage for her to walk into a board meeting a few days later and act as if nothing had been said. In some cases, however, courage can take a more basic form. Imagine being on a mission in Iraq and having to ask a male colleague to keep watch while you urinate because there were no facilities in the field for women. As Mirtha Villereal-Younger, who shared this incident, told me, "Sometimes it takes courage to speak up and ask for what you need, whatever the circumstances." In a twist on Brené Brown's famous saying "courage over comfort," Villereal-Younger's example of courage reveals that sometimes courage *is* comfort.

What these two examples reveal is that courage is multidimensional. Whether you're stepping into shoes never filled by a woman or merely showing up to do your job under less-than-ideal conditions, courage is about the ability to keep moving forward even in the face of outright hostility or risk. On this basis, I agree with Kathleen Reardon, author of the *Harvard Business Review* article "Courage as a Skill" (2007), who not only says courage can be cultivated but also argues that "those who act courageously in business settings have an instinct for opportunity."[15] While important, however, courage is a leadership attribute that is also difficult to define and rarely sufficient on its own. This may explain why it is frequently discussed in relation to another leadership attribute—resilience.

If courage is the ability to step up and face challenges, resilience is the ability to bounce back after a setback or disappointment. In leaders, resiliency is generally associated with survival, adaptation, and success.[16] It also has been shown to support one's ability to inspire and effectively lead others.[17] For many women, resilience isn't just an essential quality but the *most* essential quality.[18] This appears to hold true specifically for women leaders who face gender and racial discrimination on the job. In an article on Black and Latina women leaders, Laura Morgan Roberts and her colleagues put it this way, "In simple terms, the answer to the question of what it takes to succeed can be reduced to a single capacity: resilience. To be sure, resilience has been widely celebrated as a character virtue in the past decade, and it plays a role in every success narrative, regardless of a person's race or gender. But the African-American and Latina women interviewed seemed to rely more heavily than others on this quality because of the frequency with which they encountered obstacles and setbacks resulting from the intersecting dynamics of race, gender, and other identities."[19]

My interviews resonated with the conclusion reached by Morgan Roberts and her colleagues. One woman I interviewed, the first Hispanic woman to assume a senior leadership role in an urban police force, told me about an incident in which she was asked to "clean up" a set of long-standing issues associated with a white male colleague who had a history of bullying employees. She intervened and was widely acknowledged for facing the set of historical issues head on, having direct conversations with the offender, and consistently holding him accountable. Several months later, when incremental progress was being made, she discovered that some of her male colleagues were sabotaging her efforts and resisting changes she was initiating. Resilience, she assured me, was what ultimately helped her endure these unjustified attacks. But resilience also seems to be a critical factor in the survival of nearly all the women leaders I interviewed, regardless of their race or the sector in which they worked.

Heidi Hammel, a planetary astronomer who has worked for NASA and on the James Webb Telescope Project, reflected on the many times in her career when she has had to "get up after being knocked down and just do the next thing." Early in her studies at the University of Hawaii, she failed the oral exam for admission into the PhD program, while the other five (male) students all passed. She was singled out by her professor after the exam. He let her know that he didn't think she had the "commitment" needed to pass the exams. Despite his clear bias and her anger, she made a decision to work harder and longer hours than anyone else. Arriving at the lab at 6:00 a.m. on a regular basis and staying long after others went home, she learned a hard lesson about the need for emotional and physical resilience. It's a lesson that would ultimately serve her well throughout her career (and she did pass the oral exam on the second try).

In the case of Hammel and many of the women I interviewed, resilience thus seems to be a two-way street: resilience is what enables women to survive and thrive in traditionally male-dominated workplaces, but these environments also seem to make women more resilient out of necessity.

This leads me to a final but by no means less important leadership quality—optimism. As Ibarra, Ely, and Kolb suggest, "People become leaders by internalizing a leadership identity and developing a sense of purpose."[20] Because even individuals with a clear sense of purpose are vulnerable to other people's reactions, however, optimism is also an essential leadership trait. This isn't to suggest, though, that leading requires one to adopt a Pollyannaish demeanor.

Optimism—not naive optimism but a conviction that things can and will change—was also something that all the women I spoke to emphasized as a critical trait. "It's always in my backpack," said Hiltrud Werner, the first female on the board of management at Volkswagen International. Unsurprisingly, many of the women I spoke to who work in law enforcement were emphatic about the role of optimism. Faced with ongoing hostility from higher ups and peers, they consistently emphasized the need to remain optimistic, no matter what obstacles blocked their way forward.

Existing research in the field and my interviews for this book show that there is no question that a woman's own psychology does play a critical role in her ability to assume a top leadership role and thrive once in this position. But in contrast to much of the prevailing advice targeting aspiring women leaders, I have also concluded that it is wrong to assume that all one needs to succeed is the right mindset defined by a strong sense of courage, resilience, or optimism.

Consider, for example, how one's sense of optimism can be effectively eroded simply by one's position in an unsupportive organization. Both in my work with students in the Executive Master of Leadership Program at the Sol Price School of Public Policy and as a consultant and coach, I have repeatedly encountered women who speak of a sharp decline in their optimism as their careers have failed to accelerate as hoped. Their stories are often the same. They arrived in an organization optimistic about their professional development and opportunities for succession into leadership roles. Over time, however, the organizational culture (and often its specific treatment of women) took a toll on their sense of purpose and optimism. In some cases, these women simply burned out. In other cases, they eventually looked for growth opportunities elsewhere.

The underlying factors that can destroy optimism vary, but they are thematically more similar than different. Women are recruited into jobs that list as their requirements "demonstrated experience leading others through change" and "proven ability to work well across organizational boundaries." Once hired, however, these women frequently enter a very different cultural reality—one where their ideas are discounted, their efforts to bring about change are stifled, and their upward mobility (e.g., the ability to move from a manager role to an executive-level role) is stymied by prevailing assumptions and cultural norms. The culture of one's workplace, then, can also limit and in some cases even destroy one's optimism.

The Role of Organizations

This chapter has examined the importance of three broad categories of leadership attributes—those related to expertise, those related to purpose and self-awareness, and those related to persistence. My own research and the broader research literature on leadership suggest these attributes are essential to becoming and thriving as a leader, but there is also evidence that how these individual leadership qualities serve women differs from how they seem generally to serve men.

For example, in relation to the first set of leadership qualities discussed, curiosity and mastery, existing research suggests they are integral to rising up into a senior leadership role. Yet, as revealed in several interviews, curiosity turned out to hold another function—it helped women accept and find value in positions that represented clear demotions. Likewise, although mastery is consistently cited as a critical attribute for leaders, according to my own interviews and the broader research it seems to be a double-edged sword because highly competent women are also more likely to be negatively characterized by colleagues (e.g., several of the women I interviewed noted that even when they were promoted to executive-level positions based on their high level of expertise, they were implicitly and in some cases explicitly told that they had been invited into the room to listen but not necessarily to speak).

Similar discrepancies seemed to hold true in the case of purpose and self-awareness. Like their male counterparts, women leaders benefit from these known leadership qualities, and yet, unlike for most men, for women these attributes play as essential a role in navigating obstacles as they do in helping women identify and pursue long-term leadership goals.

The final set of leadership qualities I discussed—courage, resilience, and optimism—is also necessary. These qualities don't necessarily serve women differently than they seem to serve men, but they do appear to be most at risk of being eroded in the workplace, especially as women push forward to assume increasingly high-level roles.

So, is "leaning in" ever enough? Certainly, it helps women show up and make a case for their leadership potential, but there is only so much progress individual women can make if an organization itself continues to pose obstacles. What struck me most in my interviews is that for women, leadership attributes—their curiosity, sense of purpose, courage, and resilience—are just as likely to be used to fight off hostile attacks or to manage challenging situations as they are to help them level up. For this reason, it is not enough for individual women to cultivate known leadership qualities. The organizations for which they work also need strategically and operationally to create the conditions under which these essential leadership qualities can be consistently cultivated and leveraged. This change, dare I say, is what the call for women to "lean in" fails to address. As the following two chapters clearly demonstrate, you can lean in all you like, but if you want to move a mountain, the collective and intentional actions of others still matter a great deal.

3

The Preparation Paradox

Nearly all the women interviewed for this book started preparing for their current leadership positions decades before they stepped into them. Without realizing it, many began a trajectory toward leadership in their formative years. Still, their paths were not necessarily linear. In most cases, these future leaders were initially driven by a passion for a specific field such as science, law, or the military rather than by an ambition to reach the pinnacles of the C-suite. Another commonality among the women I interviewed is that having worked harder and pushed through more obstacles along the way than most of their male peers, these women were often over-prepared by the time they stepped into their first leadership roles. As discussed throughout this chapter, their experiences seem to be the rule rather than the exception.

Women don't necessarily wait longer to assume top leadership roles than their male counterparts (at least one study reports that they are two years younger on average[1]), but they often spend more time intentionally preparing for these roles. There are many reasons why the ascent to the top is harder for women. One known factor is that although an equal number of women and men now enter the workforce, ambitious women are still more likely to get funneled into roles with limited upward mobility, leaving them with a steeper climb from the onset.[2] Once they are funneled into job roles that are less likely to be viewed as positions leading upward, there are other consequences.

To begin, they are less likely than their male peers to be identified as having high potential to lead. They are consequently less likely to benefit from being recruited for a "high-potential" program—that is, a program designed to cultivate capabilities of potential future leaders. None of the woman I interviewed for this book mentioned being part of a high-potential program. In some cases, this likely reflects their age (high-potential programs didn't become popular until the 1990s, and many of the women I interviewed were already well into their careers by then) or their location in a sector where these programs don't exist (e.g., the military). Nevertheless, even the executive women I interviewed who started their careers in the late 1990s to early 2000s, including one who had worked for three large corporations over the course of her career, had never participated in a high-potential program or even heard about the existence of one in their workplaces.

Even when women are identified as high-potential candidates, their contributions are often undervalued or not recognized at all. Countless studies confirm that deeply ingrained gender biases continue to impact the identification of high potentials.[3] Worse yet, some studies have also found that whereas *leadership potential* seems to be more highly valued than *leadership performance* for men, the opposite holds for women. If potential matters more than performance for men but not for women, the risk is also clear: even women who clearly exhibit potential are at risk of being overlooked and excluded from the benefits awarded to high-potential men.[4]

Herein lies the *preparation paradox*. Women must overprepare for future leadership roles, but their preparation is more likely to be overlooked or minimized. In a sense, for women, preparation and even overpreparation frequently yield what may be described as a diminishing return. As will become apparent over the course of this chapter, this paradox doesn't prevent some women from rising into leadership roles, but it does mean that organizations often continue to inadvertently sideline promising women—women who might otherwise break the glass ceiling and make a significant contribution. This paradox raises a series of critical questions: How can organizations committed to putting more women and other minorities in the leadership pipeline better identify and support their future leaders? Are high-potential programs the answer, or do they end up doing more harm than good?

Early Preparation for Future Leadership Roles

Although my research never intended to focus on the impact of women leaders' formative years, nearly all the women leaders I interviewed spoke of powerful events during childhood and adolescence that influenced their leadership journey.

Consider the story of the young Janet Napolitano. Long before serving as Arizona's twenty-first governor, secretary of homeland security, and president of the University of California Board of Regents (and the first woman to serve in all three roles), Napolitano was already taking charge. As a Girl Scout, she used to take it upon herself to stuff all the other Girl Scouts' backpacks with vital implements, from maps to compasses, ensuring every detail was checked off her list before her troop set out on any hike. This might sound insignificant, but it is emblematic of the early leadership tendencies some women exhibit. For other women leaders I interviewed, leadership was something they embraced early on, out of both desire and necessity. Alma Burke, who over the course of her career rose to the rank of sergeant in the Los Angeles Police Department, first stepped into a leadership role as a child when she was called upon to look after a disabled brother and, at the ripe age of 12, to start working to help cover her family's expenses.

In addition to these early accounts of taking on leadership roles, many of the women leaders interviewed described a parent who served as an inspiration or an architect for their leadership aspirations. Some of them had fathers who worked in jobs that paid the mortgage but also found time to take an active interest in their daughters' educations. A few had fathers who occupied influential professional roles. For example, Ellen Stofan, who served as a chief scientist at NASA before becoming the first woman to serve as director of the Smithsonian's National Air and Space Museum, was first exposed to her future career when she attended a rocket launch: her father, NASA rocket scientist Andrew Stofan, didn't just take his daughter to this breathtaking event but also introduced her to space science. Not all the women who received encouragement or mentorship from parents or other family members at an early age were raised by individuals who held powerful positions, though. Maria Zuber, a prominent astronomer and vice president for research at MIT, was also inspired by a family member—in this case, her grandfather, who worked in a mine, not the aerospace industry. What mattered wasn't his position but his passion for space— one he had inherited from his own father—and his willingness to share this enthusiasm and interest with his granddaughter while also encouraging her to pursue a career he had never been able to pursue.

Not surprisingly, given that most of the women interviewed for this book were in their late forties to seventies at the time we spoke, fewer of these women cited mothers as their professional mentors because women in their mothers' generations had generally fewer professional opportunities. Many did note, though, that their mothers encouraged them throughout childhood. One courageous law enforcement leader I interviewed (who was not comfortable using her name in this book) shared several stories of her mother. As she emphasized, her mother ingrained in her a message that she could do anything she set out to do. The message would provide her with the foundation needed to enter a profession where women still face innumerable challenges on their journey to the top ranks. Likewise, Heidi Hammel, a planetary astronomer, recipient of the Carl Sagan Medal, and executive vice president of the Association of Universities for Research in Astronomy, vividly recalls one of her mother's mantras: "I didn't raise my daughter to grow up and get married." The lesson is clear: early messaging about one's potential seems to have a powerful impact.

For some women, the defining factors of their childhood were not encouragement and mentorship but rather rampant alcoholism and abuse. Far too early in their developmental journey, they were forced to learn how to take care of other family members and take charge, sometimes in the face of hostility and physical danger. Although not a background one would wish on any child, these circumstances seemed to have fueled their internal motivation and desire to change their lives and eventually make a positive difference in the lives of others. These women were often the first in their families—male or female—to attend college or leave their communities to pursue careers.

The frequency with which accounts of early life slipped into the interviews is difficult to overlook. It suggests, at the very least, that women's leadership journeys start long before they enter their professional life. After all, nearly all the women I interviewed spoke of either being encouraged early on or, conversely, being thrust into situations where they had no choice but to rise up and assume high levels of responsibility. My speculation is that both experiences instill confidence or tenacity in girls and young women, and both are arguably two of the most important factors determining ambition and drive. As it turns out, however, confidence is also fraught with gender-based assumptions.

Preparation, although partly about skill building, is also about much more. Preparation plays an integral role in women being recognized as potential leaders—a step that opens up access to further training, mentorship, opportunities, and networks. Yet even when women take their professional preparation into their own hands, their efforts are all too often undervalued or entirely overlooked.

The Importance of Being Recognized as a Potential Leader

Being recognized as a leader or future leader has been shown to have a significant double impact on whether one pursues a leadership role. First, being recognized as a potential leader is a powerful way to start crafting an inner sense of confidence and proactively cultivating one's future pathway to a leadership role.[5] Second, individuals recognized as high potentials (sometimes described as HIPOs or HiPos) become part of informal and formal leadership pipelines, which lead to in-house training, mentorship, networking, and placement in the succession-planning process. It is no surprise, then, that nearly all the women I interviewed agreed that being recognized by a person of influence was a catalyst to their eventually becoming a leader. Again, Janet Napolitano stands as a case in point.

As Napolitano would tell me in our interview, her path to leadership roles as a governor and later as the leader of one of the largest university systems in the United States started early in life. As a child, she was both influenced and encouraged by her mother, Jane Marie Napolitano, and her father, Leonard Michael Napolitano, a founding member of the University of New Mexico School of Medicine, where he later served as dean. Their mutual message, she said, was, "If you want to do something, go ahead, but you have to practice and have discipline." This mantra of practice and discipline would serve Napolitano throughout her career, but so too would being recognized as a potential leader beyond the close confines of her own family.

After completing her Juris Doctor (JD) at the University of Virginia School of Law, Napolitano clerked for Judge Mary M. Schroeder of the United States Court of Appeals for the Ninth Circuit. The position had a lasting effect on Napolitano's career. Following her clerkship, she was invited to join Schroeder's former firm, Lewis and Roca LLP. It was there that she met John P. Frank. Napolitano spoke of Frank's efforts to ensure she spent ample time in the courtroom, even at an early stage in her career. Her ability to acquire courtroom experience early on and her introduction to influential professionals would prove pivotal. Napolitano became a partner at Lewis and Roca in 1989. Two years later, she would also become part of one of the highest-profile legal teams in US history—Anita Hill's defense team in her sexual harassment case against Supreme Court judge nominee Clarence Thomas.

In many respects, Napolitano's experience is exceptional. She had parents who taught her during her formative years the importance of hard work and discipline, and she had exceptional mentorship and sponsorship in her early career. No one factor—the early encouragement, mentorship, or networking—made Napolitano into the leader she is widely known to have become, but, by her own account, these experiences did help her proactively prepare for future leadership roles.

Although Napolitano may be unique among women in general, she is not necessarily unique among women leaders—at least not among those I encountered across sectors while working on this book. Like Napolitano, many of the women had supportive parents or early-career mentors who opened doors to opportunities that eventually led to future leadership roles. However, it would be wrong to assume that all women leaders had such support. A few of the women had scrappier beginnings and rose through the ranks with sheer persistence and focus on being the best they could be. This was arguably the case for Mirtha Villereal-Younger.

As a first-generation American, Villereal-Younger found herself taking on a high level of responsibility from a young age. By 18, she was clear that joining the military would be an accessible pathway toward building a successful future. She was the only woman in her corps, and, not surprisingly, encountered sexism. As Villereal-Younger recalled, "On one occasion, a sergeant told my corps, 'You all are a bunch of ugly bitches. I wouldn't waste my time or my dick on any one of you.'" Like many of the women I interviewed who had risen to top leadership roles in the military or law enforcement, Villereal-Younger recalled these moments as matter-of-fact events but not necessarily obstructive in the long run. Although the military could at times be an outwardly hostile environment, it offered her something she had never had before. "When I joined the military, it was the first time in my life that all that mattered was what you brought to the table." Said another way, in the military Villereal-Younger's race and origins were no longer a defining factor. Her leadership potential and mastery of her craft were entirely based on her ability to perform. So long as she could successfully compete against the men in her corps and avoid being derailed by obstacles put in her path, she could continue to acquire the skills needed to advance her career and eventually assume a top leadership position.

Some women I interviewed were lucky enough to be recognized early on (e.g., Napolitano) or to stand out even among a sea of male competitors (e.g., Villereal-Younger), but others had to go above and beyond the normal call of duty to make their mark. In short, this meant stepping into stretch positions (i.e., positions that require one to engage in new or higher-level work) or, worse yet, potentially perilous positions.

Stretch Positions and Navigating Glass Cliffs

Since women are less likely to be recognized as possessing leadership potential and less likely to be automatically funneled into leadership-development programs, they must often do one other thing to establish their leadership bona fides: take on assignments that are less than ideal and, in some cases, downright risky. In fact, my research participants repeatedly shared stories of stepping into roles that were neither ideal nor prestigious nor easy but also of how doing so helped build competencies or gain access to networks that might have otherwise remained inaccessible. Here, the story of Joy White stands as a case in point.

After completing a bachelor's degree in business at Virginia's prestigious College of Mary and William, White didn't pursue an entry-level consulting position at a prestigious consulting firm such McKinsey or Bain. She instead decided to intern in the Cooper Cap Contracting Intern Program at the Space and Missile Systems Center at the Los Angeles Air Force Base. In many respects, this surprising decision would set the course for White's career. Throughout her career, she has continued to throw herself into situations and positions structured by notable challenges. As she told me in our interview, "I was moving around with my husband, an Air Force officer, so I wasn't picking and choosing my jobs, I was going in and hoping for the best. However, I learned that wherever you land, do your best and bring that upbeat attitude and willingness to take on whatever challenge. Sometimes you may feel the job is below you, and it may be. You still just step up and respect the people that you are doing the job with. You respect everyone around you."[6] White's willingness to assume a range of roles, even challenging ones, enabled her to gain a wide range of experience and acquire critical insights into the air force's inner workings. This tenacity and risk tolerance would lead her to her current role—executive director for the Space and Missile Systems Center and head of contractor activity for the US Space Force, Los Angeles Air Force Base, California.

Many other women I met spoke of throwing themselves into positions that were not only challenging but risky—roles that no one else, including male colleagues, was either willing or able to take on.

Many of these positions may be best described as "clean-up operations." In fact, women are so likely to assume leadership roles during a crisis that there is even a term for the practice: the organizational psychologists Michelle Ryan and Alexander Haslam refer to it as the "glass cliff." As they observe, although people in the general run of things "think manager–think male," during a crisis they are more likely to "think crisis–think female."[7] There are countless examples of women breaking new leadership ground in both politics and business during times of crisis. Canada's first and only female prime minister, Kim Campbell, was appointed as her party's popularity was in rapid decline and about to be all but wiped off the political map; Marissa Mayer was appointed to lead Yahoo as the company started to lose ground to Google; Mary Barra assumed leadership of GM after several product recalls; and the list goes on and on.

There are many conflicting explanations for the "think crisis–think female" mindset. Some studies have found that the skills needed to lead through a crisis include those frequently associated with women leaders. For example, a McKinsey & Company study in 2009 found that following the economic crisis of 2008, 11 percent of companies said gender diversity had gained strategic importance during the economic downturn. This likely reflects the fact that women leaders are more likely to adopt the two types of leadership behavior viewed as most important in and after a crisis: the ability to inspire employees and the ability to define expectations and responsibilities clearly and to reward employees who deliver on targets.[8] As Ryan and Haslam observe, however, other traits frequently associated with women—empathy, intuition, and creativity—may also be part of the equation. Notably, during the COVID-19 pandemic, such traits were repeatedly cited as a possible explanation for why countries led by women appeared to fare much better than countries led by men.[9] But there are also indications that the decision to catapult women into top leadership roles during a crisis may be an extension of underlying biases.

In a review of the literature, Ryan and Haslam found that leaders who hold the reins of a company through a time of crisis are far more likely to be seen as poor leaders and to be blamed for the company's problems whether they were leading the company when it went into crisis or not. This suggests that women may be intentionally put into leadership roles when an organization is in crisis with a conscious or unconscious understanding that someone will have to take the blame down the line and that it's better for the male leaders if a woman is the "fall guy."[10] Other studies suggest that women may be more likely to end up leading organizations in crisis due to "benevolent sexism." As Ryan and Haslam observe, this is a double-edged sword. Those who appoint women to leadership roles during a crisis may feel that they are doing these women a favor by offering them a challenge. In turn, in contrast to their male colleagues, women asked to step up may feel unable to refuse such offers because they would be at risk of "looking a gift horse in the mouth."[11]

Whereas Ryan and Haslam generally depict the glass cliff as a situation that carries negative consequences for women, my interviews suggest that women may have more agency in such scenarios than is often assumed and that they also frequently find ways to turn glass-cliff situations into phenomenal opportunities to gain experiences and job roles that may have otherwise remained out of their reach. In other cases, glass cliffs yield notable financial benefits. Although Mayer did resign from Yahoo after the company was sold to Verizon, she did so with a departure package that included $260 million in stocks and stock options.[12]

If women are more willing to step out onto a glass cliff and lead organizations in crisis, the practice calls another prevailing myth about leadership into question. Men are frequently assumed to make better leaders because they are more willing to take risks, and risk taking is equated with great leadership.[13] However, if women appear to be more willing to step in to lead (and may even be perceived as better equipped to do so) when risk is imminent, the assumption that men make better leaders because they are inherently more inclined to take risks no longer holds.

Can High-Potential Programs Overcome the Gender Gap in Leadership?

One doesn't have to search too hard to find articles and reports on the need to put more women into the leadership pipeline.[14] Nearly all these articles and reports recognize that getting women into the leadership pipeline is an ongoing challenge, and, interestingly, nearly all also take one thing for granted—that the benefits of high-potential programs outweigh their problems. But can we make this assumption? Would future women leaders be better served by dismantling these programs altogether?

Identifying High Potentials

Research suggests that high-potential programs consistently fail to identify the right candidates and, most notably, routinely overlook women and other minorities. Research also has shown that these programs often fail to account for people whose career paths have been less linear or predictable and, as a result, filter out more creative and innovative candidates as well as those whose atypical life experiences might bring other assets to an organization, including heightened levels of agility and resilience. Finally, considerable research suggests that when individuals know or suspect they have been either identified as high potentials and left off the list, the information can have a profoundly damaging impact on their personal sense of confidence and level of engagement. These programs have also been found to have a negative impact on organizational culture, even when they allegedly focus on promoting diversity, because they so often create yet another layer of exclusion. All things considered, high-potential programs, even if they do hold some benefits for some individuals, pose risks that directly and indirectly hinder many individuals' efforts to prepare proactively for future leadership roles.

If high potentials have all too often been selected based on subjective criteria, one might assume that access to a broader range of metrics might help organizations level the playing field for women and other minorities. Again, using different data or even a wider range of data sets to identify high potentials has proven only partially successful. As discussed at length in the later chapters of this book, performance-review data, for example, have been shown to routinely favor men over women, often for the very same reasons men are more likely to be identified as high potentials.[15] But what if you take humans out of the picture altogether?

A growing number of talent-management products on the market combine insights from industrial and organizational psychology with the powerful potential of artificial intelligence (AI) and machine learning. In theory, the turn to AI should reduce bias. After all, with AI and machine learning one can now consider millions and even trillions of data points when deciding whom to hire and promote. As a result, candidates who may have once been assessed using just a few criteria can now be evaluated in a more holistic and complex manner.[16] Unfortunately, there is little evidence that recruiters' use of AI and machine learning is eliminating bias, and some studies suggests these tools may even be augmenting existing biases.[17]

If neither humans nor machines are especially good at identifying high potentials, this raises an obvious question: Are such programs worth implementing? After all, if neither we nor AI can identify who has potential—and often in the process inadvertently stream out those who do—could it be that our high-potential programs are doing more harm than good?

How to Support High-Potential Women in the Leadership Pipeline
Beyond the challenge of rethinking when and how high potentials
are identified, there is an urgent need for organizations to rethink
how they support high-potential employees once they have been
identified as such.

In 2011, Claudio Fernández-Aráoz, Boris Groysberg, and Nitin
Nohria found, based on a survey of 70 high-potential programs
around the world, that successful programs typically include three
activities: (1) the establishment of clear strategic priorities that
guide how companies support high-potential leaders; (2) the careful
selection of high-potential candidates (and strategic management
of how the status of these individuals is communicated to others in
the organization); and (3) the management of high-potential talent, including a combination of training, coaching, mentorship,
job rotation, and retention initiatives. Yet even these researchers
stop short of describing these activities as "best practices." As they
observe, "There is no cookie-cutter method for creating a successful
program. Just as you can't lift any other people management process directly from another company, you can't assume that a high-
potential program that works somewhere else will work for you.
Your strategy and your culture influence the nature of the program
that will be most effective."[18] My own business experience and
research on talent management and equity have led me to reach
the same conclusion. I would add that it may be especially important to stop looking for cookie-cutter approaches to supporting
high-potential women. Here, it is useful to consider how standard
aspects of high-potential programs may or may not support women
and what these programs often continue to overlook.

Most high-potential programs include some aspects of mentoring. There is considerable evidence that informal and formal mentorship can help develop high-potential candidates.[19] However,
creating successful mentorship programs for high-potential women
also comes with unique challenges. There is also some evidence

that having access to a same-gender mentor may have an espe-cially powerful impact for women.[20] However, many women leaders I interviewed for this book said the most important mentors and champions they encountered were not women but men. This may reflect the fact that many of the women I interviewed work in fields where finding a woman mentor at a high level is extremely difficult if not virtually impossible, at least until the past two decades (this is undoubtedly the case for most of the women I interviewed in the military, law enforcement, and STEM fields). But there are also indications that high-potential women matched with male men-tors may have an advantage.

A Catalyst study in 2010 found that women mentors often occupy less prestigious positions within an organization and carry less clout.[21] The finding implies that mentorship programs that seek to match women with more senior women colleagues may not serve high-potential women and, worse yet, may sabotage their chances of eventually rising into senior leadership roles. Whether this is true remains debatable. What is clear is that standard fea-tures of high-potential programs need to take gender into account, but not without research. After all, even well-intentioned practices (e.g., matching high-potential women with women mentors) may not always achieve the desired effect.

Beyond the possibility that some established high-potential pro-gram activities may need to be restructured to respond to women's needs, such programs also need to seriously consider what might be missing in them. Even in the second decade of the twenty-first century, one of the significant challenges facing future women leaders is the disproportionate responsibility they continue to take for childcare and domestic labor. A Pew Research Center study in 2013 found that among parents with at least some work experi-ence, women with children younger than 18 were three times more likely than their male counterparts to believe that being a working parent had impeded their career advancement.[22] Since 2013, there are few signs that working mothers' situation has improved. During the pandemic, numerous reports found that the gap between women and men has even grown deeper. As both work and schools moved online, women who were already taking more responsibility for childcare and domestic work were "naturally" expected to do even more. The short-term consequences of this heavier load included higher levels of stress, anxiety, and burnout.[23] The long-term consequences included a narrowing of the leadership pipeline. As a McKinsey & Company study concluded in September 2020, "Due to the challenges created by the COVID-19 crisis, as many as two million women are considering leaving the workforce. If these women feel forced to leave the workplace, we'll end up with far fewer women in leadership—and far fewer women on track to be future leaders." Worse yet, the McKinsey report suggests that "all the progress we've seen over the past six years could be erased."[24] If, as suggested, work–life balance is a significant obstacle to women's career advancement and leadership pursuit, why is this issue rarely addressed in high-potential programs?

Although some high-potential programs are beginning to address work–life balance issues—perhaps because millennial men also value work–life balance more than earlier generations of men did[25]—to effectively serve everyone they need to do more than superficially recognize work–life demands. In some cases, addressing work–life balance in high-potential programs may mean rethinking these programs from top to bottom. For example, depending on the industry and company, high-potential programs often actively create avenues for promising employees to engage in overseas assignments. The rationale is that working overseas holds a host of benefits that include skill building, agility building, and networking.[26] Unfortunately, such programs have long rested on the assumption that high potentials are the sole or primary income earners in their families and therefore readily available to relocate overseas with no or few strings attached.[27] As more high-potential men enter partnerships with spouses who have their own demanding careers (careers that can't simply be dropped to accommodate a spouse's own career aspirations) and more women find themselves in the same position (i.e., balancing their career aspirations with those of a spouse), such programs naturally need to be rethought. Although high-potential men and women may benefit from overseas opportunities, the assumption that such individuals are necessarily mobile is mired in antiquated notions about gender and work. In other words, for high-potential programs to serve men and women alike, their established practices—even elements they have long taken for granted—need to be rethought and in some cases abandoned.

In the process of making changes, however, careful thought must be given to ways in which external organizational factors influence the success of any high-potential program. First, the impact of culture cannot be overstated. The values around diversity, equity, and inclusion (DEI) must be embedded in the DNA of decision making at every level. Starting at the top and cascading through to the front lines of the organization, there must be an understanding of why DEI matters and what individuals can do to diminish bias and assumptions that lead to the lessened impact of women's voices. This was precisely the point made by a veteran law enforcement leader in one of the largest precincts in the United States.

When I asked this law enforcement leader about how to promote high-potential women, she reminded me of Peter Drucker's observation that "culture eats strategy for breakfast." She added, "Organizations need to walk the walk. Women must be represented in all aspects of the organization. This includes recruitment, promotion, and leadership." But she also emphasized that changing culture in a field such as law enforcement isn't easy. "In my organization," she admitted, "there is no choice but to force change." According to her, "forcing change" has to begin by ensuring that the culture is no longer one where different standards are arbitrarily applied to women and men:

> Women have proven time and time again that they are just as
> capable as men in law enforcement and other male-dominated
> professions. However, men continue to stand in the way of the
> success of women. We've all heard the tropes about a woman's
> success in the workplace. They include: "she didn't earn it," "she
> slept her way to the top," "they lowered the standard," and the list
> goes on. It is my opinion that, if given the opportunity, women will
> meet the standard. Men just need to stop changing the standard
> after the fact.

It isn't enough just to shift the culture, either. As the law enforcement leader mentioned here and other women leaders I interviewed insisted, organizational strategy must elevate DEI as a strategic priority that channels through the system and is reinforced through metrics, business processes, training, and mentorship initiatives. All DEI efforts are for naught if the executive leadership team is not deeply committed to and accountable for outcomes that are integrated into critical success factors and compensation. Without such commitment and accountability, DEI efforts, including improved results for women and minorities, run the risk of being an empty gesture with little potential to yield results over time.

The Future Leadership Pipeline for Women

As suggested at the start of this chapter, women leaders, with few exceptions, typically spend years preparing for future leadership roles and frequently overprepare. Yet while some of those women end up in leadership roles, for many of them preparation is no guarantee that they will be identified as a high potential and reap the benefits typically associated with that designation. This statistically holds even more true for women of color. As the McKinsey & Company *Women in the Workplace 2020* report found, although one in five C-suite executives is now a woman, only approximately one in twenty-five C-suite roles are held by women of color.[28] Overcoming this prevailing paradox will take more than ambitious women willing and able to go the extra mile to develop their own leadership capacity. The *preparation paradox* will be effectively dismantled only by overhauling how organizations identify who is funneled into their leadership pipeline and how these employees are supported once they enter the pipeline.

One possible way to fix what is clearly a broken approach to building leadership pipelines may be to take the bold step of abandoning high-potential programs. If these programs continuously fail to identify high-potential women and often fail to serve women even when they are identified as high potentials, are they worth saving? As the poet and essayist Audre Lorde famously said, "The master's tools will never dismantle the master's house."[29] Lorde most likely wasn't thinking about corporate high-potential programs when she wrote this line, but if each organization, including a corporate organization, can be understood as one "house" among many that form a culture or community, her words are arguably still relevant to this discussion. Simply put, sometimes social transformation isn't contingent on fixing existing programs or institutions but rather on dismantling existing structures and finding an entirely new way to move forward.

My suggestion that high-potential programs may not be worth "fixing" is likely to come as a surprise to some business experts and leaders, but I'm certainly not the first person to suggest that they may do more harm than good. More than a decade ago, Douglas Riddle, then the director of the global coaching practice at the Center for Creative Leadership, warned in the *Harvard Business Review* that high-potential programs, if not properly managed, risk producing a workplace culture dominated by arrogant prima donnas.[30] But my own critique of high-potential programs isn't just that they risk excluding deserving employees while elevating the status and egos of undeserving ones. The real problem with these programs is that they are based on false assumptions about the leadership journey, especially in the twenty-first century.

Nearly all high-potential programs are based on the premise that high potentials (i.e., future leaders) are already on the leadership path early on in their career, even at the entry level. Although this may be true for some people, it doesn't necessarily hold true for all or even most individuals, nor does it make much sense in today's job market.

First, different people peak at different moments in their life and career cycle. As a consultant and a coach, I have experienced this firsthand. Indeed, I have worked with dozens of individuals who didn't even realize they had leadership potential when they were in their twenties or early thirties or hadn't yet landed in the career where they would eventually rise into a leadership role.

Second, we know statistically that people are changing jobs and careers more often now than ever before. The IBM Institute for Business Value found that an estimated one in five workers changed jobs in 2020, with Gen Z (33 percent) and millennials (25 percent) accounting for more than half of the job churn.[31] Similarly, another recent study carried out by Prudential found that one in five workers changed their line of work entirely in 2020, with half of respondents saying the change was permanent.[32] The pandemic was clearly a factor in this movement, but even before the pandemic hit, millennials were more than three times as likely than older generations to report changing a job in the past year.[33] Given that the majority of job changers and career changers are younger than 40, there is also reason to believe that this trend will continue over the coming decades, again calling into question the value of high-potential programs that tend to be based on the assumptions that one's career path is a linear and predictable trajectory.

Finally, and of specific significance given the topic of this book, women are still more likely to exit and reenter the workforce than men due to pregnancy and childcare obligations. Although some of these exits and reentries are made by choice, this is certainly not the case for all women. They also often struggle to reenter at the same level they were at when they exited and even to reenter the same career. There is also evidence that the more hierarchal a sector is, the more difficult it seems to be to leave and reenter. This issue was raised in my interview with Joy White, executive director of Air Force Space and Missile Systems Center. White emphasized that for both civilians and military personnel, having a family remains a major obstacle to women's advancement in the air force.

> In the air force, they won't typically start looking to advance a woman until she is already a major or lieutenant colonel. But by then, there are not that many women in these roles because in the early phases we lose a lot of women as they decide to have families. On the civilian side of the air force, if we can offer women flexibility at that stage, it can make a huge difference. But the reality is that the senior ranks, when you start to look around, there just aren't a lot of women who can be promoted on either side because we tend to lose them when they are younger.

For all the reasons outlined here, the assumption that one's leadership journey is a linear progression that starts with an entry-level position and ends up in a leadership-level role is extremely dated. In fact, it is a premise that never held true for all workers and now doesn't hold true for a growing number of workers regardless of their gender.

If organizations want to transform high-potential programs, they can't focus only on doing a better job at identifying high-potential employees. They also have to find a way to build programs with multiple entry points (e.g., programs that have opportunities for entry-level workers as well as for individuals who are already well along in their career or pursuing a career pivot). This restructuring will not be easily accomplished. It will mean radically rethinking the competencies needed for the future of work and what a typical leadership career path looks like. It will also require organizations to completely rethink which skills are transferable and from what contexts. At its most progressive, this restructuring would entail building a high-potential program that might, for example, be able to recognize the high potential of a woman who has just reentered the workforce after spending nearly a decade working at home caring for a young child and running a freelance consulting business (I did this at one point in my career, so I can attest to the fact that this combination of tasks is not easy and does help build a wide range of skills). To reach this point, however, we first need to undo the entrenched scripts that continue to structure nearly all workplace cultures. The next chapter discusses how to do this important work.

4

Entrenched Scripts and Double Standards

It would be nice to believe that if you lead with a compelling vision, identify champions of change in your organizations, and consistently communicate a strategic message, it is possible to drive the cultural shifts needed to support rising women leaders. Unfortunately, even a clear vision and best practices seem to be no match for the deeply pervasive cultural scripts that continue to structure organizational life.

These cultural scripts can hold a purpose. At their best, they offer templates for what is acceptable and how one should communicate and behave in the workplace. On this account, these scripts help workplaces, which are always complex social microcosms, function smoothly. But they are also deeply embedded in the bones of nearly all organizations and tend to calcify over time. As a result, they are frequently rife with gender-based assumptions and other biases from earlier periods. When women—or, for that matter, men— break from the scripts laid out for them (those organizationally viewed as "appropriate"), there are consequences. A woman who adeptly follows a scripted part for a man, for example, will likely experience a remarkably different reception than a male colleague playing the same part. When double standards continue to mar women's upward mobility in the workplace, these scripts are largely to blame.

This chapter focuses on four scripts that seem to have an especially powerful grip on workplace cultures even in the twenty-first century: the scripts that structure verbal communication; the related scripts that govern silent communication (e.g., body language, proxemics, and even style); the scripts that control displays of authenticity and emotion; and, finally, the scripts that influence displays of confidence and humility. As will become apparent over the course of this chapter, these scripts are not only deeply entrenched but also rarely broken, so that women who do break them are left to navigate workplace cultures on their own and without a rule book on how to play the game.

The Communication Trap

When women don't speak up, they are characterized as demure and passive. When they do speak up in a direct manner, they are all too often characterized as aggressive and self-interested. To make matters worse, there is no obvious or easy way to overcome this communication trap. It is no surprise, then, that most women leaders know this trap only too well.

The stereotype about women who are too direct and aggressive is alive and well. Women in male-dominated fields walk a thin line between stating their views assertively and being perceived as a "bitch" or "nasty" (as Donald Trump characterized Hillary Clinton).

As I learned many years ago, when interacting with men in powerful positions, a woman is best served by being exquisitely aware of her presence, tone, and attire. Although in some organizations this need for hyperawareness has tempered over the decades, being the first or only woman in a room full of men still comes with a need to be highly observant of organizational dynamics and intentional about all facets of communication.

One of my most memorable moments of navigating the chasm that often exists between how women and how men are required to communicate occurred in the early 2000s. One day, while we were enjoying lunch at a restaurant overlooking the Atlantic Ocean, a lower-level executive at the company where I was a member of the C-suite surprised me when he asked, "Hey, honey, how do you think your mother would feel if she knew you were having lunch on the Red Neck Riviera"? After taking a thoughtful pause, I laughed off the discomfort and quickly changed the conversation. In one fell swoop, he had drawn attention to my age, gender, and religious and cultural background. This was one of the most stunning microaggressions I had ever experienced in the workplace. My colleague seemed to assume that it was his natural right to belittle me in a professional setting, even though I had more power in the organization than he did since I was in the C-suite and he was a regional publisher. Yet he was clearly unconcerned about the potential consequences of his comment to me. Although not apparent in the moment, inappropriate remarks such as this one taught me a crucial lesson about leadership. Because others saw my gender and other identity markers first, my words were regularly at risk of being eclipsed, but following the script available to my male counterparts also wasn't an option for me. This is the essence of the communication trap that women in nearly all workplaces fall into. As explored over the course of this chapter, overcoming this specific trap remains one of the most vexing challenges facing both women who aspire to lead and organizations that aspire to support them. One also doesn't have to go far to find examples of the double standard that women face when it comes to communication in the workplace.

One woman leader I interviewed—an executive of a multinational company—described an initial orientation to her new position on the board of management (in Europe, this is equivalent to serving in the C-suite). Of course, she was delighted to receive the invitation and was confident that the position was a good match for her. She was familiar with several members of the management team and confident that her peers would welcome her in her new role. It was only after she arrived that she realized that as the only woman on the board she was perceived to be part of a peer group but was expected to listen without sharing opinions. In fact, at least one man on the board even explicitly told her, "You can come in, but you can't speak." Despite her prior experience with certain members of the executive team, she discovered that as soon as she was appointed to a new and all-male context, the rules changed. She was welcome, but her contributions were not.

In another interview for this book, the chief of police of a mid-size US city recounted a time when she was invited to speak on a panel with the local mayor. The two had been invited to a community meeting to openly discuss policing and community safety. They listened to residents' concerns, respecting their diverse opinions and demonstrating interest in potential solutions. When the evening's program was brought to a close, however, the moderator thanked the mayor and never acknowledged the chief of police's presence or contributions to the discussion. Given her years of dealing with outright aggression, she took the omission in stride. After all, to speak up would be to risk sounding "whiny." It was easier to roll with the discomfort and understand that it is par for the course.

In some instances, not only are women leaders expected to remain silent or are overlooked when they do speak up, but even the possibility that a woman might speak also remains unimaginable.

One of my interviewees is an established scientist who has published many highly regarded research studies. As is the custom in most STEM fields, she uses only her initials when authoring journal articles. Many years ago she was invited to Russia as a guest of the Kremlin. Her peers were shocked when they saw she was a woman when she showed up. They had been reading her papers for years and assumed she was a man. In this case, she was permitted to speak and was heard but likely only because she was assumed to be a man prior to arriving. In this case, the default use of initials and not first names in scientific publishing enabled her to develop a career and reputation without being judged according to gender-based assumptions.

The personal accounts of the communication trap shared in my interviews for this book were by no means an exception. They mirror decades of research on gender, communication, and leadership that also consistently show that women both struggle to speak up in professional contexts and, more importantly, are frequently misheard when they do.

Although research on women's communication styles dates back at least a century, with the rise of women's liberation in the late 1960s and the subsequent move to secure a place for women across the ranks of the workforce, the need to understand gendered communication styles took on increased urgency over time. From the 1950s to the 1970s, a growing body of research sought to shed light on how communication might be impacting women's mobility in the workplace. However, much of this research continued to reproduce established assumptions about how women communicate or ought to communicate. For example, many of the earliest studies on women's communication in the workplace seemed to presume that women are more open than men in their communication style and therefore necessarily stand in sharp contrast to the stereotype of the "strong, silent male."[1] Early studies also frequently reinforced the idea that women are socially oriented in their communication style, whereas men are more task oriented—that is, compared to men, women are less likely to get to the point and stay focused in conversations.[2] A few positive stereotypes were also reinforced in this early research, including the perception that women are warmer and better equipped to express emotions in their communications.[3]

One of the first major studies to compare the communication styles of male and female managers was published by John Baird and Patricia Hayes Bradley in 1979. The study—based on the results of an 18-item questionnaire distributed to 150 employees at three organizations (a midsize hospital, the clerical department of a midsize manufacturing firm, and the production line of a small manufacturing company)—offered support for the already deeply held assumption that women and men communicate differently and therefore have inherently different leadership styles. Among other key findings, Baird and Bradley noted that women managers were more likely to share information and come across as friendly and approving. On this basis, the researchers concluded that the implications for leadership were profound. "In the situations examined here," they observed, "females generally did not enact a 'male role,' but instead communicated in ways markedly different from the behaviors exhibited by male managers. In communication content, women statistically exceeded men in giving information, stressing interpersonal relations, being receptive to ideas, and encouraging effort." They also noted that some qualities—those generally linked to leadership—were more likely to be exhibited by male managers: "In communication style, males generally exceeded females in dominance, being quick to challenge others, and directing the course of conversations, while females scored higher on showing concern and being attentive to others."[4]

Over the next decade, studies reinforcing Baird and Bradley's findings continued to be published. The question that was generally overlooked was why women's and men's communication styles appeared to be so different and deeply entrenched. This question was finally tackled in a sustained way by the sociolinguist Deborah Tannen, who would eventually publish one of the first books on gendered communication in the workplace, *Talking from 9–5* (1994).

In many respects, Tannen's book continued to support earlier findings on gender and communication in the workplace. For example, Tannen also concludes that women are more likely than their male counterparts to ask questions and even admit to not having all the right answers. But *Talking from 9–5* also shed light on another issue—the fact that the rules of the game (i.e., communication expectations) are remarkably different for women and for men and that these rules seem to take shape decades in their lives before they enter the workforce.

As Tannen discusses at length in her study, the communication trap that structures women's experiences in the workplace doesn't begin in the workplace but rather in early childhood. Boys' groups, she observed, tend to be more hierarchical (e.g., in sports there is nearly always a team captain, and no one disputes the need for such a role). Girls, by contrast, tend to be socialized and encouraged to communicate in a profoundly different way. According to Tannen, girls are more likely to play one-on-one or in small groups. As a result, if a girl takes the lead—that is, assumes power—she is quickly called out as self-centered or bossy. Simply put, for girls, fitting in means finding ways to share power, collaborate, and on a linguistic level take turns in conversations. In boys' early play, there appears to be a tacit understanding that there will always be followers and leaders. As a result, boys aren't necessarily expected to share power or take turns in conversations. These ingrained lessons about how to share power and communicate also don't end with childhood. Indeed, as Tannen observed, communication lessons learned in childhood are replicated throughout life, including in the workplace. When it comes to leadership, this replication creates an obvious and significant obstacle for women.[5] Simply put, the communication patterns that girls and young women are encouraged to adopt are largely incompatible with the communication patterns associated with leaders. To rise as leaders, then, women effectively need to unlearn early lessons on how they should communicate. Likewise, their male colleagues need to unlearn expectations about how women should communicate.

Whether the problem is hardwired (i.e., women and men have inherently different communication styles) or, as Tannen suggests, social (i.e., girls and boys are socialized to communicate in different ways), the consequences appear to be the same. As women work their way up to higher levels of an organization and the gender balance shifts (i.e., men outnumber women), their learned communication style becomes increasingly out of sync with the established norms at those higher levels. To thrive, women bear the onus to adapt—for example, to ask fewer questions, make more definitive statements, and, of course, avoid apologizing or sounding hesitant. For the woman who manages to adapt, of course, there are still hurdles to overcome. Because boys and men aren't just socialized to communicate in a certain manner but socialized to *expect* girls and women to communicate in a certain manner, when women adapt to fit into the communication norms of a male-dominated environment, they run another risk—of not meeting expectations for how women should speak. This is the communication trap that nearly all women leaders must navigate by virtue of gender and organizational level. It's also a trap that continues to have consequences.

Although Tannen's book on gender and communication in the workplace first appeared in 1994, her insights are regrettably still applicable. Consider, for example, the highly conflicting perceptions of communication that ended up dominating Ellen Pao's high-profile lawsuit charging gender discrimination at Kleiner Perkins Caufield & Byers in 2015. During the 24-day trial, reams of evidence were presented by both parties attempting to prove or disprove that Pao had been denied promotions based on a systemic pattern of gender discrimination. Some of the most contentious evidence presented during the trial included Pao's past performance reviews. On the one hand, the performance reviews painted the picture of a woman who was consistently outspoken and overly aggressive. Among other comments, they stated that she was "dismissive, occasionally publicly, of peers," "pushing too hard to establish herself, instead of being collaborative," and had "'clashes' or issues with many different partners."[6] On the other hand, they offered a sharply conflicting account of her communication style. As one partner concluded, Pao lacked what it took to become a full partner in the firm because she was "passive, reticent, waiting for orders with her relationships with CEOs." Pao told the *New York Times* in an interview carried out shortly after she lost her case, "Everything was conflicting: You talk too much/not enough. You're too data-oriented/you don't bring enough information. . . . There was no consistency."[7]

The lack of consistency to which Pao refers is a recurring theme across workplace domains that researchers continue to grapple with. In 2017, Elizabeth McClean, a professor of management at the University of Arizona, and her colleagues carried out a study examining the impact of leaders using promotive versus prohibitive language—that is, language that presents helpful ideas for the future versus language that points out problems without necessarily offering solutions. In the first study, 196 working adults, 38 percent of whom identified as women, were enlisted to listen to four recordings: the first was of a male using promotive speech; the second was of a female using promotive speech; the third was of a male using prohibitive speech; and the fourth was a female using prohibitive speech. McClean ensured that the scripts for the promotive and prohibitive speeches were identical for the male and female speakers and that they were delivered in a similar fashion. When the 196 participants were asked to assess the leadership qualities of the different speakers, men using promotive speech were viewed as better leaders and earned more respect than men using prohibitive speech. However, there was no difference in the assessments of the women using promotive speech and the assessments of the women using prohibitive speech. Regardless of what they said or how they said it, women were not viewed as better leaders or given more respect than their male counterparts. In a separate experiment, McClean repeated the study but this time solicited the participation of 187 cadets at the United States Military Academy's Sandhurst Military Skills Competition. Again, the women who adopted a promotive style saw no benefits in terms of how they were perceived as leaders.[8]

As McClean and her colleagues conclude, "Not considering peers' perspectives of voice paints an incomplete picture of the benefits and detriments that people might consider in their voice calculus when deciding whether or not to speak up." After all, as their study demonstrated, "while voice may positively relate to higher positions in a social hierarchy, not all voice exerts the same effect."[9] Simply put, communication strategies that appear to garner positive effects for men often don't do the same for women. For this to change, however, we need to stop focusing on changing how women speak and focus instead on how both men and women *listen* to their female colleagues. Most organizations unfortunately don't invest in training men and women to listen differently—that is, to become aware of their biased perceptions of voice. My own speculation is that if more organizations started to invest in listening training for women and men rather than communication workshops for women, we would be more likely to see measurable organization-wide changes. Until this happens, the communication trap described in this section is bound to persist.

More Than Words

Communication is rarely just about words. Personal characteristics from body size to body language to sartorial choices also appear to interfere with how women are heard in the workplace.

Take the rather obvious issue of height. Although there are certainly exceptions, most women are shorter than most men. One's height shouldn't have a direct bearing on communication, but research suggests that it does. Studies have found that from an early age children already appear hardwired to perceive taller individuals as more dominant than shorter individuals.[10] Other studies have found that dominant men are also routinely assumed to be tall, even when they are not.[11] For many women, even those who have invested in an entire closet full of heels, height alone continues to pose a barrier in the workplace, specifically on the path to leadership. But size isn't the only thing that matters.

For many decades, research supported the idea that eye contact is an important element of effective leadership. Much of this research pivoted on the fact that eye contact tends to be associated with several key leadership qualities, including decisiveness and dominance.[12] Eye contact is also frequently viewed as a powerful prosocial behavior that plays an integral role in establishing connections between speakers. Based on these findings, one might conclude that women aspiring to lead should use more direct eye contact in their workplace communications. When women do, however, this encouraged form of nonverbal communication may or may not serve them. If overused, eye contact can come across as threatening. To make matters worse, research suggests that eye contact seems to be interpreted differently based on the gender of who initiates the contact, suggesting that when eye contact is deployed in the workplace, there is no guarantee it will be interpreted identically across genders (or for that matter across cultures).[13] In short, this communication strategy seems to serve men, at least in some cultural contexts, but doesn't necessarily serve women in most contexts and can even backfire when they deploy it.

In the workplace, similar challenges arise in relation to proxemics and touch. When men use touch in the workplace—let's say, by offering a pat on the back—it is nearly always a top-down gesture that affirms their dominance. When women use touch in the workplace, it is more likely to convey sympathy or compassion or to be used to forge a connection. In other words, the same gesture (a pat on the back) may be used, but why it is being used and how it is perceived by the recipient can be remarkably different depending on who uses it.[14] As with eye contact, if there is an existing "rule book" on touch, it seems to be profoundly structured by gender. However, whereas men are given clear guidelines, women are essentially left to navigate the workplace without the guidance afforded to their male counterparts. Interestingly, though, this is not why Carol Kinsey Gorman, who has written extensively about body language in the workplace, suggests that the lack of women CEOs "has everything to do with body language."[15]

Citing a study by a team of University of Delaware researchers, Gorman notes that the real problem may not rest on how women communicate verbally or nonverbally but rather with how people react when they do communicate. In the study in question, researchers found that when women speak up in meetings, "negative nonverbal affect cues [by others at the meeting]—frowns, head shakes, eye contact avoidance, and so on—are displayed, processed, and often mimicked by the entire group to produce a less-than-positive consensus about the value of the woman's contribution." Worse yet, unlike conscious responses (e.g., people cutting women off when they attempt to speak in a meeting), these negative nonverbal cues generally go unchecked. After all, although one might be able to call out a colleague who consistently cuts off his female colleague, calling out the same colleague for frowning or rolling his eyes is far more challenging. Gorman cautions her readers that this specific study has limits and further notes that it is not just men who appear to unconsciously react negatively to women asserting leadership qualities—women are just as likely to express such silent displays of disapproval. Gorman somewhat optimistically concludes, "The power of nonverbal communication lies in its unconscious nature, so simply discussing this issue and bringing it to awareness will decrease its frequency and help nullify its effect."[16] But if awareness were enough, would we still be grappling with these problems even after decades of workplace education on gender and leadership?

This brings me to a final form of silent communication that may appear superfluous but certainly is not so for most women: one's workplace uniform.

In 2010, UBS (better known in the United States as the Swiss Bank) issued a controversial 43-page manual on how to dress in the workplace. Unlike many workplace dress manuals, UBS offered sartorial advice to both their male and female employees. As clearly outlined, suits must be dark gray, black, or navy blue. Socks should be black and knee-length to avoid any skin exposure. Men should avoid using tie knots that don't match the shape of their face or body shape. Facial hair, including fashionable stubble and beards, are strongly discouraged, but having a good haircut, updated once a month, is encouraged because, as the manual explains, "studies have shown that properly cared-for hair and a stylish haircut 'increase an individual's popularity.'" For women, UBS offered somewhat more predictable advice—for example, no short shirts or nail art, but "light makeup consisting of foundation, mascara and discreet lipstick" was given approval based on the conclusion that it can "enhance your personality." After the manual received far more media attention than anticipated, UBS issued a statement clarifying that it was intended only for a small percentage of frontline staff in Switzerland. What was most notable about UBS's manual was the organization's strong defense that, like it or not, clothes not only make the man (or woman) but also make the business. As a UBS spokesperson said at the time of the controversy, "The goal is for clients to immediately know that they are at UBS when they are entering the bank." In other words, without supplying uniforms, the organization was asking employees to adopt one, notably at their own expense but within UBS's very clear constraints.[17]

Although most organizations stop short of offering detailed advice on everything from tie knots to makeup, most do have expectations about how employees should or can show up in the workplace. Like other scripts, including those that govern verbal and nonverbal communication, having guidelines on what one should wear to work isn't an inherently bad idea. It can even make life and work easier for employees. As I did the research for this book, for example, nearly all the military and law enforcement leaders I interviewed talked about the powerful impact of working in uniform. Many felt that their uniform helped them feel and stay in charge, even when facing hostility on the job. When interviewing a lieutenant colonel in the US Army, I noticed that she mentioned her uniform several times and its powerful impact on her ability to occupy her position of authority. Prior to joining the army, she had endured years of physical and emotional abuse at home and as a result grew up suffering from low confidence and a profound lack of self-esteem. As she recounted her many accomplishments in the military, she acknowledged the power of working in uniform. "I feel confident while I'm in uniform. I feel as if I have a voice. When it's off, I still struggle with the imposter syndrome and a lack of confidence that I can't shake."

If the uniforms worn by women in the military and law enforcement appear to serve as a type of shield—something that effectively neutralizes their gender, at least on the job—for most women workplace uniforms are conversely yet another source of unnecessary stress. The hypervisibility of one's body and attire are something most women learn by trial and error, often by ending up in an awkward circumstance and sometimes through informal guidance offered by friends and colleagues. The pressure to blend in is par for the course, especially for women working in more conservative professions. What kind of jewelry is acceptable? Should a dress always be accompanied by a blazer? Is it permissible to wear bright colors? What happens if you show up to a meeting and your workplace attire doesn't align with that of the men in the room? One of my interviewees, a well-known geophysicist, told me about arriving at a global conference in a foreign country and realizing she had brought the wrong clothes. During a brief break, she ran out to buy a new suit in an attempt to better blend in among her colleagues. I, too, have scoured the shops of many cities and towns looking for "appropriate" pieces of clothing so I could fit in. Few women ever discuss these incidents, but they are more commonplace than one might expect. Notably, I have yet to meet a man who has ever felt the need to run out between sessions at a conference or a break between meetings to purchase a more appropriate tie or new pair of shoes.

Research suggests that how women look, both their physical appearance and fashion choices, does affect how they are perceived at work far more directly than it does men. One study in 2011 found that when the study's participants were instructed to focus on a subject's appearance, women but not men were viewed not only as less competent but also as less warm and even less moral.[18] Other studies have found that in various professional contexts women are also more likely than men to be judged based on their appearance.[19] There is further evidence that women are more likely than their male counterparts to assume that how they dress will impact how they are perceived in the workplace and affect their upward mobility. The Center for Talent Innovation (now known as COQUAL) found in 2011 that "women, in particular, believed that dressing the part was a vital factor in attaining success: 53 percent of them felt aspiring female execs needed to toe a very conservative line, avoiding flashy makeup, plunging necklines, too-short or too-tight skirts, and long fingernails." Women surveyed for the study also believed that appearance engenders self-confidence, a core leadership trait. However, the Center for Talent Innovation study further found that although women believe that their sartorial choices matter, knowing what to wear remains a mystery. As Sylvia Ann Hewlett, the center's founder and one of the study's authors, observes, "Women, certainly, struggle more than men to achieve the look of leadership, a factor that contributes to their overall stall in middle- and upper-middle management. On the one hand, they're told to conform; on the other, they're advised to stand out. They're told to downplay their sexuality but warned against coming off as too mannish and threatening." In short, not unlike the verbal communication rule book that tells women they should speak up if they want to be recognized as a leader but shouldn't speak up too often or too loudly, the rule book on how women should dress is rife with contradictory messages and conflicting advice. Whether one adopts a power suit or a "power dress," which the *Wall Street Journal* described in 2019 as a garment that "makes you feel confident, and allows you to take ownership of your femininity,"[20] the problem remains the same. Whereas men face few choices on the fashion front and have a clear rule book on how they should dress depending only on context, women face many choices, little clarity about what may or may not meet their organization's largely unspoken expectations, and more dire consequences if and when they fail to make the right choices.

Authenticity and Emotional Intelligence

So far, this chapter has examined areas of workplace life where women are frequently penalized for conforming to the established rules because, for them, playing the game correctly means deviating from gendered norms or, conversely, struggling to identify the rules when no clear guidance exists. But what happens when women, especially women leaders, do what women supposedly already do well? For example, there are now growing calls for leaders to show up as more authentic and emotionally attuned. Since women are frequently praised on both accounts,[21] one might assume that this shift in perspective on leadership should work to women's advantage. As the following discussion reveals, however, even when it comes to leveraging supposedly inherent strengths, entrenched workplace scripts often leave women at a distinct disadvantage.

First, consider the growing interest in authentic leadership. Since Bill George published *Authentic Leadership: Rediscovering the Secrets to Creating Lasting Value* in 2003, which called on a new generation of leaders to demonstrate a greater passion for their purpose, hundreds of articles have been published on the importance of authentic leadership. George's primary thesis on leadership is simple—if you want to lead effectively, you have to walk your talk. In other words, you should both believe in and embody your mission. George would later elaborate on his call for authenticity in *Discover Your True North* (2007). In an excerpt from this second book published in the *Harvard Business Review*, George puts it this way: "You can learn from others' experiences, but there is no way you can be successful when you are trying to be like them. People trust you when you are genuine and authentic, not a replica of someone else."[22] But it would be wrong to assume that George's call for authenticity has targeted all leaders or necessarily resulted in women leaders being rewarded for behaving authentically.

In 2015, three Australian researchers put George's authenticity thesis to the test when they compared the media coverage of two CEOs of national banks, one male and one female, during the global financial crisis. As the researchers found in their comparative study on media representations of Mike Smith, the CEO of ANZ, and Gail Kelly, CEO of Westpac, authenticity seemed to be deeply structured by gender-based scripts. "Doing authenticity," they concluded, "meant doing gender in line with stereotypes of what it means to be a man (independent, strong, active and decisive) and a woman (nurturing, caring, outgoing and communal) in the Australian context."[23] For this reason, although both Smith and Kelly appeared able to leverage their authenticity, it was only to the extent that they adhered to certain preexisting gendered scripts. As a result, when Kelly exhibited decisive behavior—for example, when she raised interest rates in December 2009, before Australia's other three major banks made the same move—the media framed her decision as hasty. In fact, compared to ANZ's CEO, Kelly's proactiveness was generally met with negative media attention. As the researchers observed, "Kelly's decisiveness did not work to de-gender discourses that were previously seen as exclusively masculine. Instead, Kelly's authenticity was called into question."[24] On this basis, the researchers conclude that because authenticity, like gender, is socially constructed, it seems to work only when it aligns with the assumptions regarding one's biological sex (i.e., women can use authenticity to their advantage only if it is viewed as stereotypically feminine).

The interviews carried out for this book led me to reach a similar conclusion: authentic behavior works to a woman's advantage if it is perceived as feminine, but when women behave in a way that appears "masculine," the opposite holds true. Consider the still-outrageous pay differential between men and women. In negotiating salary or a compensation package, women, unless they are well trained in negotiations, often prematurely agree to a lower salary, assuming that if they push harder, they will be viewed as unlikeable or antagonistic. This exact situation was illustrated during my conversation with a renowned scientist (who didn't want her name used in relation to this anecdote), who recounted a salary discussion in which she was told the offer was nonnegotiable. The end of this story is self-evident—she ended up signing a contract that set her salary well below the norm given her level and accomplishments. She discovered later—in conversations with male colleagues—that the nonnegotiable status was a false claim. The unanswered but obvious question is what would have happened if she had pushed back? Although she may have been true to herself in this pushback moment, being true to herself—that is, assertive—may still have backfired. The fine line between speaking one's truth and adapting to perceived expectations illuminates the nuances that surround one's ability to truly be authentic in the workplace.

The scientist's experience was echoed in the work history of another interviewee—an executive leader in the public sector (who was also unwilling to go on the record with this specific anecdote). As this woman recounted, when she was direct or definitive about her viewpoints or suggested a plan of action, she was consistently labeled "bitchy." Rather than remain true to herself, she adapted her performance to "soften" her image in the workplace. Specifically, rather than state facts and plans of action upfront, she started to preface statements with a personal story. By telling personal stories, she appeared more authentic and relatable. In truth, however, being assertive and decisive was still as much a part of her authentic self as the stories. Ironically, she had to adopt a performance that didn't come to her naturally just so she could appear authentic. But if authenticity is a valued twenty-first-century leadership characteristic, is it not time to make explicit the value of accepting an entire range of authentic performances, even those that may not align with one's gender? Here the pandemic stands as an interesting case in point.

Early on in the pandemic, there was praise for at least a few female leaders' handling of the crisis, especially when they displayed authenticity in a way that aligned with gender expectations. New Zealand's prime minister Jacinda Ardern, for example, received considerable praise when she broadcast a press conference from her own home just moments after putting her toddler down to bed.[25] Yet beyond a few standout accounts of women leaders' authentic and empathic responses to the crisis (such as the widely publicized Ardern press conference), most stories about authenticity and leadership during the pandemic largely focused on men. In March 2020, for example, just a few days after Ardern's widely reported home press conference, Bill George published an article in *Working Knowledge*, a publication connected to the Harvard Business School, in which he proclaimed, "Now is a time for leaders, particularly authentic leaders, to step up to the challenges and inspire their organizations to help the world work its way through these difficult times." George offered a "personal 'Heroes List' of authentic leaders who are making a difference in overcoming the challenges of COVID-19." Amazingly, he didn't include a single woman in the list, despite the fact that there were certainly women leaders on the political stage, in public health, and in business making headlines for their early response to the pandemic.[26] George is clear to state that his list is personal, but the list is notable if only because it begs a rather obvious question—Why did George, who is an expert on authentic leadership, fail to notice the performance of women leaders? Because these leaders aren't on his radar or because being authentic is something more likely to be taken for granted among women leaders?

Authenticity isn't deeply structured by gender alone, though. In the workplace, race is also something that appears to impact one's ability to show up in an authentic way—that is, in a way that is true to one's core self. Here, Tina Opie's research stands as a case in point. Opie and coauthor Katherine W. Phillips find that despite hair being integral to one's expression of self, "historically, Black women's choices about how to wear their hair has been informed by societal pressures to adopt Eurocentric standards of straight hair." In fact, in several studies, including clinical studies, they found that Black women who show up in the workplace with Afrocentric hairstyles still risk being viewed as and penalized for presenting as overly dominant and unprofessional. However, Opie and Phillips further emphasize that it doesn't have be this way. "Ursula Burns, the only Black CEO of a Fortune 500 company," they observe, "exemplifies how Afrocentric hair does not have to hinder professional success." They further maintain, "CEO Burns' embrace of her Afrocentric hair conveyed her comfort with her authentic self. Such authenticity has benefits for the individual, as well as, the organization."[27] Opie and Phillips's study confirms that although authenticity is a desirable trait among leaders, it come with different "rules" based not only gender but also on race, making it more difficult, if not impossible, for Black women in particular to leverage their authenticity in the workplace.

Notably, this conundrum was often noted in my own interviews for this book. Take, for example, Tiffany Felix, the senior vice president of environmental health and safety at ViacomCBS. A Black woman executive at one of the nation's largest media companies, Felix is someone who has often found herself working in environments where she is in the minority in terms of not only her gender but also her race. I personally became acquainted with Felix when she was a student in the Executive Master of Leadership Program where I teach, so I know her to be an incredibly authentic person—someone who never hesitates to speak her mind. When asked about her experience in different organizations, however, Felix was clear that when she chose to leave an organization, it was either because the organization no longer could offer her opportunities for advancement or couldn't provide a climate in which she could be herself. When asked to reflect on the impact of the latter situation, Felix emphasized, "To not be able to show up as your authentic self is very, very damaging." But authenticity isn't the only issue at stake here.

Here, it's useful to broaden the discussion to emotional intelligence (EQ), which Daniel Goleman and Richard E. Boyatzis break down into four domains—self-awareness, self-management, social awareness, and relationship management—with 12 more granular competencies under each domain.[28]

Since the early 1990s, there has been a growing recognition that great leaders nearly always have high EQs and that a high EQ may even be more important than possessing a high IQ. Given that women are consistently viewed as possessing higher levels of EQ than men and are sometimes viewed as better leaders due to their high levels of EQ, one might assume that women have naturally benefited from the recognition of EQ as a valued leadership trait.

Beyond a few small gains (as discussed in chapter 1), however, women still occupy just a small fraction of top leadership roles.

The psychologist and researcher Tasha Eurich suggests that there may be an explanation for why women leaders haven't been able to leverage EQ to secure top leadership roles. The problem simply may be that women tend to underestimate how others view them. For example, in one study cited by Eurich, when women and men were asked to predict how a supervisor might rate EQ, women's predictions were three times lower than men's predictions. In reality, superiors tend to give women higher EQ ratings than men. On this basis, Eurich observes, "the ability to correctly predict how others see us, often called meta-perception, is an important aspect of self-awareness. And indeed, when women underestimate how others view their contributions, they may unintentionally hold themselves back."[29]

A related problem, according to Eurich, is that women are also less likely than their male counterparts to receive useful feedback. "When women *do* receive feedback," she notes, "it's typically less specific than feedback given to men. This has profound consequences: studies have shown that when women receive vague feedback, they're more likely to be assigned lower performance ratings." But, as Eurich notes, a lack of specific positive feedback can also put women leaders at risk. After all, if women leaders aren't being validated for possessing certain traits, such as a high EQ, they may not fully leverage such traits to their advantage.[30]

Although these explanations are compelling, there may be another reason why EQ seems to be overindexed as a strength for male leaders and underindexed for female leaders. When male leaders show up as sensitive and self-aware, they tend to be praised for exhibiting depth and relatability. When female leaders do the same, they are sometimes viewed as overly emotional, which is one reason women have historically not been viewed as potential leaders.

Women's authority often requires establishing a certain degree of professional distance. As a result, the same action might be considered appropriate and deeply empathetic when enacted by a male leader but come across as inappropriate, meddling, or simply unhinged when enacted by a female leader. Take, for example, the unusual decision made by Colonel Mark Anarumo, the president of a Norwich University, a military college in Vermont, after a cluster of COVID-19 cases emerged on his campus in early 2021. Worried about the mental health of students living and studying in quarantine for weeks on end, Colonel Anarumo, a 50-year-old air force veteran, decided to move into a single room in a campus dorm. For a university president, it was an extraordinary act of empathy, even if he did spend only five days living in the dorm (by contrast, his students were in quarantine for weeks). The unusual act was also long enough to garner Anarumo a feature article in the *New York Times*.[31] One has to wonder, however, what the media coverage would have been if Kathleen McCartney, the president of Smith College, or Christina Paxton, the president of Brown University, had moved into a dorm on campus because she was worried about the mental health of students during lockdown. Would these women university presidents have been praised for their empathy and compassion, or would the gesture have undermined their authority or, worse yet, simply be viewed as peculiar and inappropriate?

This is where authenticity and EQ arguably also differ in important ways. Women get points for being authentic but only to the extent that the form of authenticity they show adheres to gender-based assumptions. In the case of EQ, the opposite seems to hold true. Women leaders appear to be able to leverage their EQ, but if they overindex on EQ—that is, come across as *too* empathetic or compassionate—they risk losing the distance perceived to be important to maintain their authority as leaders or are viewed as "too soft." Thus, while women leaders are frequently lauded for their authenticity and EQ, their authenticity works only when they remain stereotypically feminine, and EQ seems to work best when they skew toward a stereotypically masculine performance instead.

Humility and Confidence

The final set of convoluted workplace scripts this chapter attempts to untangle comprises those that tacitly structure displays of humility and confidence.

Like authenticity and emotional intelligence, humility has become a catchphrase in leadership theory in the 2000s. As Jim Collins, author of *Good to Great* (2001), argues, "Level 5 leaders"—that is, those leaders who aren't just good but exceptional—are invariably humble leaders.[32] Since Collins's publication hit the best-seller list in 2001, countless articles have been published on humility and leadership. In general, advice on the topic seems to boil down to just a few key points. Best practices in leadership tell us that humble leaders aren't selfless, but they are more self-aware. This means they learn from mistakes, welcome criticism, and empower their employees to do the same. Like other newly promoted leadership strengths, however, displays of humility also seem to present a double-edged sword for women. When women follow Collins's script for how to act as a humble leader, they don't always get the same reception or results.

A study published in the *Academy of Management Journal* in 2012 found that female leaders generally felt pulled between the need to behave humbly and the need to establish their reputation for competence. As the researchers found, "It seemed that with regard to humility, female leaders operate in a more narrow range of acceptability, feeling pressure to be a strong leader on the one hand and a humble female on the other." As one of the study's participants explained, "What I've learned is that if you're a female, people expect different things. I think humility is expected more for a female leader than a male leader, but they need to see you as competent too. As a woman leader, that's a complex one for me." Interestingly, a male leader interviewed for the same study seemed to agree that for women being humble comes with fewer rewards:

"In our society, women are expected to be humbler. Males are given more credit when they are humble."[33]

In my interviews with women leaders, this contradiction was a recurring theme. It's also something I have frequently confronted in my own professional life. As an executive in charge of all back-office functions except finance at a large media company, I was told that several board members were not comfortable with the information technology (IT) department reporting to me because of my lack of experience in this discipline. Their preference was for me to assume coleadership with the CEO, who coincidentally also did not possess any IT experience but was a man. I complied and with humility accepted their illogical request. Caught between the desire to be viewed as a good team player and a competing desire to call out the board members on their obvious gender bias, I chose the former route. Here, it would be difficult to imagine a man ever ending up in this situation, let alone responding with humility if asked to share the post with someone else who also did not possess any IT background. But in one of the many catch-22s for women, if too much humility threatens to undermine women's authority, displaying too much confidence also comes at a high cost.

Despite the ample evidence that not all women lack confidence and that women of color are particularly inclined to want to "lean in" at work (64 percent of Black women in the United States say their goal is to make it to the top of their profession, which is nearly double the number of white women who hold this goal[34]), there is still a prevailing perception that women lack confidence. Indeed, lack of confidence is frequently cited as a key factor preventing women from obtaining top-level leadership roles. In many respects, this is the thesis of Sheryl Sandberg's *Lean In*—the more confident women become, the more likely they will rise. Popular websites such as Arianna Huffington's Thrive Global also reinforce this message by regularly publishing articles with headlines such as "7 Secrets for Female Leaders to Boost Self-Confidence" and "How to Close the Women's Leadership Gap by Raising Confident Girls." Yet research suggests that being or even just appearing more confident in the workplace isn't necessarily advantageous for women.

Victoria Brescoll from the Yale School of Management carried out a study in which groups of male and female students were given an opportunity to rank a fictitious CEO who, they learned, talked more than others during the meeting. When told the CEO was female, both male and female participants viewed the CEO as less competent than when they were told the CEO was male. The study suggests that displays of confidence—for example, holding the floor in a boardroom—are perceived in remarkably different lights by one's peers and followers depending on who is making them.[35]

A study carried out by Leslie Pratch and Jordan Jacobowitz in 1996 reached a similar conclusion. In this case, the researchers used a variety of existing assessments (e.g., Jackson's Personality Research Form and Raven's Advanced Progressive Matrices) to predict peer ratings of leadership at the end of a nine-month leadership-development program. The study found that both women and men in the program expected women leaders to engage in "expressive, relationship-oriented behaviors such as consideration of others, playfulness, and emotional expressiveness." Other common leadership traits, such as independence, decisiveness, and ambition, which are more likely to be associated with displays of confidence, seemed to have an adverse effect when displayed by women. As the researchers concluded, "It appears that women are not allowed to display these qualities if they are to succeed as leaders."[36]

Again, the findings of these studies resonate with my own experiences and the qualitative research carried out for this book. When women are either overly humble or overly confident, they are penalized. As a result, they must strike a balance—often adopting a neutral stance—to survive and succeed. But this dance is a delicate one that requires women to constantly monitor when humility will be viewed as an asset and how to demonstrate confidence without intimidating others.

Organizational Interventions

As this chapter has demonstrated, aspiring women leaders must navigate multiple scripts—even contradictory ones—to rise to the top. They are expected to assert themselves and speak up, but when they do, they are penalized for failing to adhere to gendered norms. Women are also expected to hold the room like men, but when they do, their actions are frequently misinterpreted. Furthermore, women are sometimes encouraged to leverage supposedly inherent strengths, such as authenticity and emotional intelligence, but on a conflicting gender-based axis (i.e., authenticity works when they stick to a feminine script, but emotional intelligence seems to work best when they adopt what is perceived to be a stereotypically masculine performance). Likewise, women are told to be humble but are judged as incompetent or weak if they are viewed as overly humble; and, conversely, they are told they lack confidence but are frequently penalized when they display confidence. Simply put, in the workplace women are expected to follow two types of scripts simultaneously—one for adhering to gendered norms and another for adhering to leadership expectations. Simultaneous adherence to these scripts is a high-wire balancing act that must also fully align with one's organizational culture. It is thus not entirely surprising that organizational attempts to address the obstacles facing women who aspire to lead often continue to fail and sometimes do more harm than good. A recent attempt to support aspiring women leaders at a US branch of Ernst Young (EY) illustrates why and how institutional efforts often go wrong.

In June 2018, an EY branch in New Jersey hired Marsha Clark, a third-party consultant, to deliver an in-house training for the women on its team. EY's leaders in the New Jersey office presumably had good intentions when contracting with Clark to offer her Power-Presence-Purpose workshop. But the response to the workshop was anything but positive. The workshop led to an internal controversy at EY, and when a document from the workshop was leaked to the media, it led to a public-relations disaster for the consulting firm. What went wrong during the EY workshop exposes the complexity of addressing entrenched scripts and double standards in the contemporary workplace.

Clark's presentation first drew attention to the "invisible rules" that structure workplace communication. As the participants learned, women tend to keep their communications brief, wait their turn to speak, and phrase their thoughts and ideas as questions. According to participants who attended the workshop, however, Clark didn't offer any strategies on how to challenge these rules. Indeed, some EY participants later claimed that they were essentially told that women are generally better off adhering to these entrenched scripts since deviating from them can result in conflicts. Although this may be true, many of the women in the workshop found the advice disempowering. Among other snippets of advice, the workshop participants were also told to avoid looking directly at male colleagues and to sit at an angle from male colleagues in meetings; as one participant wrote down during the workshop, "Don't talk to a man face-to-face. Men see that as threatening." Even more controversial was the workshop's advice on nonverbal communication. EY's women were told to look "healthy and fit" and to make sure they have a good haircut and manicured nails. They were also advised to avoid "bottle blond," plunging necklines, flashy jewelry, short skirts, and, above all else, skin. Skin, they were cautioned, should always be avoided since it "scrambles the mind," making it difficult for colleagues, male and female, to focus. However, the key takeaway from the workshop wasn't that EY's women should abandon a feminine presentation in the workplace. Clark also cautioned that they will be penalized by women and men alike if they don't adhere to feminine stereotypes or, worse yet, choose to act overly masculine instead.[37]

Given that only 5 percent of the total number of male or female applicants are hired at EY, it seems reasonable to conclude that all the women who were invited to participate in EY's Power-Presence-Purpose workshop in 2018 were exceptionally qualified and had already exhibited high potential. As one of the top consulting firms in the world, EY is already a powerhouse of intellectual capital. So why were these bright and talented women being told by a consultant hired by EY to avoid speaking up, looking at their colleagues in the eye, and sitting directly across from them at a table? Although some women who attended the workshop were grateful for the advice, many others were angry. One employee, who wouldn't give her name to the media due to fear of retaliation, said the unsolicited advice on how to communicate and what to wear made them "feel like a piece of meat."[38]

What reports on the EY workshop controversy tended to overlook is that Clark, although clearly being used as the scapegoat in this case, was never the source of the problem. Perhaps what the EY controversy ultimately reveals is that even when one tries to navigate the conflicting rules governing women's workplace presentation, communication, and performance and to offer a coherent strategy on how to succeed, it is difficult, if not impossible, to present a winning formula for all women. Another potential problem with Clark's workshop is that it targeted only EY's female employees and thereby implicitly and by some accounts explicitly seemed to place the onus solely on women to bring about organizational change. But given that gender discrimination in the workplace is often connected to low levels of psychological safety, one might conversely argue that, depending on the workplace, mixed-gender workshops may not be the right response either.

I mention the EY incident here not because it is unique or because I necessarily agree with the EY employees' dismissal of Clark's efforts but because it garnered considerable attention. Every year across the United States and around the world, organizations with the best of intentions host similar workshops. Some of these workshops, like Clark's, target women and purport to offer advice on how women can navigate the contradictory scripts that govern nearly all workplaces. Others focus on women and men and aim instead to raise awareness of inherent biases. Neither attempts to empower women nor attempts to sensitize men seem to yield the desired results. In surveying the DEI training that had been given at 829 companies over 31 years, Frank Dobbin, Alexandra Kalev, and Erin Kelly found in 2007 that such training had no positive effects at the vast majority of companies.[39] More than a decade later, Dobbin and Kalev published a related article with findings that may be even more disturbing. A number of recent studies on antibias training rely on an implicit association test before and after to determine whether unconscious bias is affected by DEI training. In a meta-analysis of 426 studies, Dobbin and Kalev found "weak immediate effects on unconscious bias and weaker effects on explicit bias," but they also disturbingly discovered that "a side-by-side test of 17 interventions to reduce white bias toward blacks found that eight reduced unconscious bias, but in a follow-up examining eight implicit bias interventions and one sham, all nine worked, suggesting that subjects may have learned how to game the bias test."[40] Worse yet, further research has found that the effects of antibias training seem to dissipate within a few days. So could DEI training be doing more harm than good? And if training isn't the solution, what is?

Driving Cultural Change

Culture is the foundation for organizational norms; that is, culture determines what counts as acceptable behaviors in an organization. Regardless of the definition, culture encompasses every act tolerated in a system. It includes written and unwritten rules and prescribed behaviors. When a company is seeking to transform its culture, close attention must be paid to the assumptions and beliefs underlying statements about what is valued and aspirational. Is an organization prepared to embrace different leadership styles? Would a woman who is a great listener and prefers a collaborative approach to decision making be perceived as powerful as a male with similar attributes? Likewise, would a woman who is straightforward, speaks her mind, and respectfully lets others know when boundaries have been crossed be viewed as "bitchy" or confident? Such granularity might sound like a waste of time and energy, but when it comes to shaping organizational culture, the "devil's in the details." It is far too easy to craft values and statements about prescribed behaviors without diving into the minutia. For this reason, in patriarchal systems—most organizations are patriarchal even if they don't see themselves in this light—the challenge of hiring and promoting women into leadership roles cannot be the sole responsibility of a hiring manager. The decision must start at the very top and be reinforced throughout the culture. Simply put, new strategies and processes need to be adopted and then embedded into the fabric of the organization.

To begin, organizations need to recognize that women can't be the sole agents of change. Structural change, especially change that starts at the top, is critical. For example, consider the "rule of three": when at least three women are on a board of directors, organizations start to see cultural change, including more appointments of women leaders.[41] What holds true on boards also seems to hold true on other workplace teams. The presence of more women has a stacking effect that seems to drive and sustain broader changes. But hiring more women and minorities is just the first step.

For real change to happen, organizations also need to do more than get more women on boards and in the C-suite—they need to recognize that women are not a homogenous group, even if nearly all women CEOs are a homogenous group. As noted in chapter 1, among the 37 women who made the Fortune 500 list in 2020, none was Black or Latina. This means that addressing the gender gap in leadership also means adopting an intersectional approach. To date, this is arguably where much of the existing research continues to fall short. Getting women in the C-suite is an admirable goal, but if all future women leaders are imagined to be white cis-gendered heterosexual women from a narrow range of backgrounds, the problem will persist.

As discussed throughout this chapter, organizations also need to start viewing women's strengths as strengths rather than deficits and to do so early in the career cycle. Among other things, this may mean paying more attention to people who are listening rather than taking up speaking time in meetings. It may also mean radically rethinking the criteria used to funnel employees into early management positions.

Finally, organizations, even those with the best of intentions, may be best advised to accept that the timeline for real change is likely not months or years but decades. As emphasized throughout this chapter, the scripts that need to come undone to disrupt the workplace and pry open more opportunities for women aren't scripts that we encounter for the first time in the workplace—they are scripts we learn as children that pervade all aspects of our lives. This is not to say that organizations can't lead change, but leading change without a massive societal shift will likely prove to be an uphill battle. On this account, however, there may be at least some hope on the horizon.

There are encouraging signs that the very youngest members of the workforce may drive future change and be more amenable to letting go of gender-based scripts than previous generations. Whereas only 12 percent of Boomers know at least one person who uses gender-neutral pronouns to refer to themselves, more than one-third of Generation Z (people born between the mid-1990s and the early 2010s) say they do.[42] Generation Z isn't just less attached to binary understandings of gender. It is also the most ethnically and racially diverse generation in history. On this basis, a Deloitte study on Generation Z wisely cautions organizations "not to fall for the myths and stereotypes: Whether you're talking about gender and ethnicity or modes of learning, Gen Z refuses to fit into neat little boxes."[43] The workplace's youngest employees also may be arriving there with a different perspective. Raised primarily by members of Generation X, they are also more likely to have grown up with two working parents, including mothers who experienced firsthand the unforgiving barrier of the glass ceiling.

It is still far too early to predict whether the open-mindedness, diversity, and cynicism of the youngest members of the workforce will have a measurable impact on workplace cultures over the coming decades. What is clear is that to retain this somewhat unique generation, workplaces will have to bend to accommodate their radical new norms that seem to apply to gender and other identity categories as well as to workplace expectations. Here, it is worth noting that tensions between the youngest members in the workplace and their "higher ups" are already on the rise. In early November 2021, a telling headline in the *New York Times* simply read, "The 37-Year-Olds Are Afraid of the 23-Year-Olds Who Work for Them."[44] Interestingly, among other concerns is the fact that younger employees seem bolder about asserting their needs, less interested in corporate hierarchies, and more willing and able to demand that their bosses pay attention to equity issues. If millennial leaders respond to rather than retreat in the face of these demands, this could be the start of the sea change for which we have been waiting.

5

Building an Ecosystem of Support

One assumed reason why women don't obtain top positions is that they lack access to informal networks. In some respects, this is true. One of the leaders I interviewed for this book, the president of a highly ranked research university, shared an account that illustrates just how difficult it can be for women to access the spaces where networking often occurs.

The incident in question took place at the president's first meeting with her university's board of directors. Ironically, the board meeting was scheduled to take place at a private club for men—and no, it wasn't the 1960s but the 1990s when this incident occurred. When she arrived at the venue, the doorman kindly informed her that "ladies" had to use a separate entrance. Rather than inciting an argument, she permitted the doorman to escort her to the basement entrance reserved for the spouses and invitees of club members. The board meeting proceeded without any reference to the earlier fiasco. Upon completing the agenda at the end of a long day, the president thanked everyone for a productive meeting, recounted the unusual experience she encountered when entering the building, and in a business-like manner informed the board they would never convene at this location again. As president of the university, it was her right to request a new and gender-inclusive venue. Had she not been in this executive tier, though, she would have found herself where many women do—outside and with no obvious way to penetrate the highly fortified world of male-dominated networking venues.

Networking opportunities often continue to shut out potential leaders either explicitly or implicitly. From fraternity networks that are still restricted to male members to networking clubs that may now be inclusive on paper but until the late twentieth century excluded an entire range of individuals (in many cases not only women but also men of various racial, ethnic, and religious minorities), places where leaders network frequently remain off-limits to some either explicitly or implicitly. As a result, operating in these spaces, even if possible, often continues to be a struggle. In many cases, however, the exclusion isn't about an organization's membership rules or history. Women (and even men who don't fit certain stereotypes and expectations of the prototypical male leader) are also frequently excluded because the networking event is simply an awkward or unwelcome cultural fit for them.

At a venture-capital firm that had finally recruited its first woman partner, the firm invited all its partners, including its new woman partner, to engage in a weekend of deer hunting at a remote lodge in Colorado. Just one month after her appointment, this invitation posed a serious dilemma for her. If she bowed out—in part because she was an environmentalist and vegan from the Northeast who had never picked up a hunting rifle in her life—she might compromise her future at the firm. Even if she remained a partner, she suspected her absence would be noticed and work against her. If she said yes, she would have no choice but to go on a shopping trip to Dick's Sporting Goods, buy a new wardrobe she had never anticipated purchasing or needing (and certainly not for a work event), and grin and bear an awkward weekend of male bonding and animal killing in the wilderness. Either way, she knew that this networking opportunity would likely never work to her advantage.

Despite such incidents, women can and do find ways to formally and informally network with colleagues and build robust support networks in and beyond the workplace. Emerging research suggests the networks women build are often more effective and longer lasting than those built by their male counterparts.[1] In this chapter, rather than focus on how women are sometimes still shut out of networking opportunities, I focus on how successful women leaders go about building a complex ecosystem of support that includes formal channels (e.g., organizational mentorship and coaching programs); informal channels (e.g., informal mentorship relationships and relationships with champions or personal advocates); private channels (e.g., spouses and friends); and personal channels (e.g., self-support and self-efficacy). As will become apparent, women who rise to the top nearly always have benefited from not simply one but all or most of these support channels. Although dismantling male networks and sites of support (e.g., fraternities, all-male clubs, etc.) may appear to be a pressing goal, this chapter suggests that a more productive approach may be to proactively foster existing sources of support for women, especially at the midmanager level, where so many women's careers seem to stall.

Formal Channels of Support

The first and probably most widely recognized support networks typically originate in the workplace. These networks often include formal mentorship and coaching programs. Although not all these programs are effective, there is compelling evidence that with the right oversight they can have a significant impact on women's careers.

Formal Mentoring Programs

In surveying the results of existing studies on mentoring programs in four nations (the United Kingdom, the United States, Canada, and Australia), Lisa Ehrich found in 2008 that "mentoring can yield both career developmental outcomes such as salary increases and promotion as well as psycho-social supportive functions such as counseling and friendship. Mentoring can also provide valuable opportunities for learning and growth."[2] However, Ehrich further notes that some mentoring programs are more effective than others, and this seems to hold true whether they target women or men. Specifically, she found that three factors affect the outcome of mentoring programs.

First, mentors need to be conscious of the extent to which they are directing the mentoring relationship. This is important because when mentees have more agency (i.e., can direct the relationship), the outcome of the mentorship relationship is more successful.[3] Building on David Clutterbuck's research, Ehrich further emphasizes that the more didactic the mentor is, the less empowering the experience will be for the mentee. Although she does acknowledge that there may be times when mentors need to set the agenda, especially at the start of the relationship, she concludes that the best mentors are those who empower mentees to take the lead. "Effective mentors," she writes, "will need to be open and aware of the way they communicate with their protégés and seek to encourage protégés to take responsibility, make decisions, and define the parameters of the relationship."[4] A final factor that appears to have a profound impact on the success of a mentorship relationship concerns power. Best practices, Ehrich concludes, argue for an orientation to mentoring that is developmental, has learning as its focus, and is based on power sharing or "power with" rather than on hierarchy or "power over." However, there are some exceptions. While sharing power makes sense in the case of "developmental mentoring" programs where the focus is on learning, it may not in the case of "sponsorship mentoring" (a subject I discuss in greater detail later in this section) because in the latter case, the goal is to use one's position to bring about gains for one's mentee.[5]

With few exceptions, mentorship seems to benefit women and even to benefit women more than it benefits men. There is also evidence that mentorship programs may be especially vital for women in specific circumstances. Margaret Linehan and Hugh Scullion, for example, have found that women often benefit significantly because they are more likely to lack access to informal networking opportunities. In their study of female global managers, they noted that a lack of effective networking was "a key barrier to the development of female global managers, and in particular, that the continued lack of access to male networks is particularly damaging as men continue to hold power in most organizations." Yet, as they further discovered, mentoring may be one approach that can help women overcome this stubborn workplace barrier. On this basis, they conclude, "while mentoring relationships may be important for men, they are even more essential for women's career development as female managers face greater organisational barriers to career advancement."[6]

In addition to evidence that mentoring programs may be particularly important in certain industries and workplace cultures (e.g., global firms), there is evidence that some mentorship models may be more beneficial than others. As already noted, there are generally two different approaches to mentorship—developmental and sponsorship. Whereas developmental mentorship focuses on behavioral change at the level of the mentee (e.g., helping the mentee develop the knowledge, skills, or executive presence needed to rise into higher-level positions), sponsorship mentorship leverages the mentor's status to advance the mentee's status (e.g., to move the mentee into a higher-level position). Marilyn M. Helms, Deborah Elwell Arfken, and Stephanie Bellar conclude that sponsorship may be especially important for women because it not only prepares the protégé for potential opportunities but also seeks to persuade others (both inside and outside of the organization) to offer pathways of opportunity to the protégé. In a qualitative study of women who had been mentored, they further discovered that offering women access to mentoring may be more likely to have a long-term impact on organizations because "almost 90% of the participants who were mentored stressed the value of their mentoring and asserted the importance of continuing to mentor others once they themselves have been mentored and benefitted from it."[7]

Here, the experience of one of my interviewees, Tiffany Felix, senior vice president of environmental health and safety at ViacomCBS, stands as a powerful example. Like many women, Felix hasn't had a linear career trajectory. She started her career in a corporate setting, left that setting when she had her children and worked as a consultant for nearly a decade, and then returned to it. As she noted in our conversation, after she worked as a consultant—an opportunity that enabled her to expand and grow at her own pace—the return to the corporate world was difficult. "In corporate settings, someone is always telling you that 'this is your box.' When I did consulting, there was no box—it was entirely open—which is why I probably learned more working as a consultant than I have in any other role." Unwilling to remain confined to a box, when Felix returned to the corporate world, once an organization started to stifle her progress, she would look for a new opportunity. This is how she eventually met someone who would ultimately serve as her champion. "All my roles, all of my experiences of elevation," Felix said, "have had something to do with people moving me up." Felix explained, "At one point, I wanted to get out of NBC, so to the surprise of many of my colleagues, I interviewed for a director position at American Apparel. In the end, they said I was too qualified and put me into a SVP [senior vice president] role instead. That's where I met Craig, a white male who was the chief of human resources at the company at the time. In the end, Craig would take me into three different companies as he also moved around. We no longer work together, but he was definitely someone who has championed me at different points in my career."

This leaves one final question: Is the cost of mentoring programs worth it? Mentoring programs nearly always come at a cost both to the organization and to the individuals who participate. Upfront costs to organizations include lost productivity due to the time allocated for the mentor and mentee to convene. Upfront costs to the individual also include time, which can be especially difficult to spare for women, including female mentors, because they generally have greater demands on their time outside of work (e.g., at home and on the parenting front). On this basis, Helms, Arfken, and Bellar further note that mentoring may even pose risks for women because "women are in high demand as mentors, but women who mentor downward too much may impede their own career advancement."[8] Given the strong evidence that mentorship programs are an effective way to support women seeking to move up in an organization but may come at a cost to women, including female mentors, organizations are well advised to consider how to invest in mentorship programs so that both women mentees and mentors benefit alongside the organization. One solution may be to proactively encourage more men to mentor women rather than other men. Another obvious organizational intervention is to begin to incentivize and reward executives who engage in mentorship, especially the mentorship of women and other minorities.

Coaching

In the mid-1990s, when I began my career as an executive coach, most people assumed I was referring to some type of athletic endeavor. Since these early days, the field has exploded, matured, and become commonplace across sectors. Coaching is practiced by individuals whose backgrounds often vary widely, from seasoned C-level executives and psychologists to applied behavioral scientists and spiritual advisers. Given the diverse types of coaching available, it is difficult to define it as a practice. However, the following description offered by Anthony Grant, a member of the council of advisers at Harvard's Institute of Coaching, does a good job of illuminating coaching's central tenets. As Grant argues, at its most basic coaching is "a collaborative solution-focused, results-orientated and systematic process in which the coach facilitates the enhancement of performance, life experience, self-directed learning and personal growth."[9]

Although coaching may be difficult to define, a growing body of research suggests that it does make a difference. According to the Institute of Coaching at Harvard University, 80 percent of people who receive coaching report increased self-confidence, and more than 70 percent report improved work performance and relationships as well as more effective communication skills.[10] Given the known impact of coaching, organizations are increasingly viewing it as a good investment likely to yield a positive return and even something worth cultivating in-house.

My extensive experience in the field also supports the idea that coaching yields positive outcomes in most circumstances, particularly when a client is motivated to change and has some degree of insight. If the intended outcome is enhanced self-awareness, then the client must be able to spot maladaptive behavior and be inspired to change. But can coaching, like mentorship, help women attain and/or retain leadership roles?

As discussed in earlier chapters, women often arrive in the workplace with behaviors and assumptions that date back to their childhoods. Some of these behaviors and assumptions are no longer productive and may even undermine their ability to assume higher-level leadership roles. As Ronald Burke and Deborah Nelson observe in *Advancing Women's Careers* (2002), some behaviors reinforced in girlhood directly work against one's leadership aspirations.[11]

For example, have you noticed how often women say "I'm sorry" for no apparent reason? It may be a small thing, but as Burke and Nelson suggest, it is just such learned tendencies that consistently undermine women's leadership potential and their position as leaders. Having witnessed this in my own graduate classrooms over the years, on one occasion I placed a jar in the middle of the room. Every time a woman started a statement with an apology, she had to put 25 cents in the jar. The clink of pocket change added humor to the exercise, but it also helped make a critical point: women routinely apologize more than men, and it comes at a cost to their leadership. Of course, you don't need a jar of coins to modify this behavior—a good coach can help manifest this type of behavioral change.

To this day, I'm grateful to the coach I hired when I became the chief learning officer and only woman in the C-Suite of a large media company. It didn't take long to discover that the culture was deeply patriarchal, steeped in tradition, and slow to change. The adage "it can be lonely at the top" took on new meaning and soon led me to hire an external confidante and highly seasoned coach. This might be the wisest professional development expenditure I have ever made because this individual accelerated my socialization process and sense of self-efficacy, which were critical to my success within the organization. I clearly benefited from coaching, but should I have had to pay for the coaching out of pocket? Candidly, this is where organizations could make a notable difference for women and other minority leaders, but it also appears to be where many organizations continue to fail women.

First, there is evidence that women are less likely than their male counterparts to receive coaching. A survey of 3,000 US-based human-resource professionals found that one-fifth indicated that women don't receive the equivalent amounts of coaching as men at the managerial or leadership levels.[12]

Second, there is also strong evidence that although coaching is often approached as a gender-neutral activity, the best coaching programs take gender into account. As Deborah A. O'Neill, Margaret M. Hopkins, and Diane Bilimoria emphasize in their study, although there is evidence that coaching can have a positive impact on women, executive coaches of women must recognize the unique organizational and societal strictures that face women pursuing leadership opportunities. Specifically, they observe that women may face challenging contexts, work–life integration concerns, and career impacts at different life stages than men. "Given these three core factors," they conclude, "women have distinct developmental needs as they seek to establish their leadership presence composed of self-confidence, self-efficacy, influence, and authenticity," and "coaches of women need to understand the nuances in women's careers and lives to effectively help them realize their ideal vision of themselves as leaders."[13]

A final problem entails the cost associated with coaching. Most executive and leadership coaches charge anywhere from $250 to $500 per hour. The most established and well-known coaches often charge much more. If coaching costs are relatively high, it likely reflects the fact that many executives have a dedicated coaching budget. In other words, they aren't paying—their organizations are. For managers, it is a different story. Many managers have access to leadership training but not to individual coaching. Because women managers tend to make less than their male counterparts (one study published in 2019 found that women at the highest managerial levels experience the most significant pay gap, earning on average $48 per hour less than their male counterparts[14]), the need to support coaching for women at the manager level may be especially important. Indeed, I would argue that funding coaching for women managers may be the most important and impactful intervention that organizations committed to supporting future women leaders can make.

Informal Channels of Support

Beyond formal mentorship and coaching programs, informal forms of mentorship and simply having a champion—that is, someone who recognizes your capabilities and pushes you forward, especially when you're questioning your own potential—are critical. Unfortunately, there is little quantitative or qualitative data on the impact of having an informal mentor or champion because these relationships tend to happen organically and even outside the workplace. From my experience and the accounts of the interviewees, having the support of a champion can be a pivotal point in one's career.

Fiona Ma, California's state treasurer, credits her mentor and champion—the late Senator John Burton—with helping her craft the principles that still guide her career and with supporting her desire to run for local office earlier in her professional life. Ma is vocal about the impact Senator Burton had on her commitment to helping the underserved and doing the right thing, even if she was the lone voice in the room. As discussed in an earlier chapter, Janet Napolitano also credits an early mentor and champion—John P. Frank, the lawyer who helped shape the argument in the landmark *Brown v. Board of Education* case and later became a partner at Lewis and Roca LLP—for helping promote her early in her career. When Frank passed away in 2002, Napolitano, who was then running for state governor of Arizona, told the *New York Times*, "He really worked to open the legal profession to women and minorities."[15]

To appreciate why informal channels of support matter, it is useful to consider the emerging research on friendship in the workplace. Although it is certainly the case that friendship can at times lead to exclusion in the workplace (i.e., create networks that make it difficult for women and other minorities to thrive), friendship isn't necessarily negative. As Marissa King, a professor of organizational behavior at the Yale School of Management, has consistently found in her studies on workplace friendships, "The research is pretty clear that workplace friendships have enormous benefits. Having social support from coworkers reduces stress, helps reduce burn-out, improves efficiency and productivity, and increases employee engagement." But King also has found that "women are much more likely to keep their work relationships and their personal relation-ships separate." This approach, she notes, carries many advantages, such as maintaining a better work–life balance, but, according to King, it also means "women need to network twice as hard as men to build work relationships, because they're not working and hang-ing out at the same time." The solution, King suggests, "is to create environments where everybody can feel authentic, where they can show up and be their authentic selves."[16]

One possible way to extend the known benefits of informal work-place networks is to build affinity groups across workplace func-tions, divisions, and even locations. For example, for many women of color, being the only woman of color in the room is a familiar experience. Given this situation, looking for support beyond their current workplace function, division, and location is frequently necessary. Fortunately, as more work moves entirely or at least par-tially online, the opportunity to build affinity groups in new ways continues to expand. Zoom meet-ups and Slack channels can allow minorities working in the same organization but in entirely differ-ent functions, departments, or locations to easily connect and build informal networks of support. Given the low cost and ease of build-ing these online networks, they are a rather obvious way for organi-zations to help transform their organizations for women and other minorities.

Private Channels of Support

While I was working on this book, Kamala Harris became the first woman to assume the role of vice president of the United States.

Although most attention has been on Harris, her spouse, Doug Emhoff, has also garnered considerable notice and not necessarily because he was particularly visible during Harris's campaign. As he reportedly said early in the campaign cycle in 2020, "I'm just, you know, a husband, and I'm here to tell people why I love Kamala."[17] Emhoff's visibility was magnified later when it became clear that he was permanently leaving his law firm not only to avoid any potential conflicts of interest but to fully embrace his new role as "Second Gentleman" of the United States. Emhoff hasn't been immune to criticism for his decision to step back as his spouse assumed one of the most powerful leadership roles in the nation. Although Harris clearly got where she is on her own merits, the question remains— Could she have done it without a supportive spouse, one willing to curtail his own career ambitions?

Anecdotally and statistically, one's choice of a spouse does appear to make a difference, especially for women leaders. In 2017, Avivah Wittenberg-Cox published a frank article on women leaders and their spousal choices in the *Harvard Business Review*. "Professionally ambitious women really only have two options when it comes to their personal partners," Wittenberg-Cox writes, "a super-supportive partner or no partner at all. Anything in between ends up being a morale- and career-sapping morass."[18] Based on my own experience, I think Wittenberg-Cox is right. Every married woman I interviewed for this book eventually talked about the critical role their spouses played throughout their careers.

Maria Zuber, for example, couldn't have been clearer with her recommendation, "Marry a good guy!" She recalled her husband's flexibility and support as being instrumental during the years in which they were raising children and she was building her career. Among the women I interviewed, she was one of several who had husbands who had picked up and moved several times to support their wives' careers. Coco Brown, founder of the Athena Alliance and former board member of the IBM company Taos, recalled some very trying phases in her career and the many changes her husband made, including leaving his job, to support her and their family.

On the flip side, when women don't have a fully supportive spouse, they often find themselves struggling to keep up. I still recall a time when my son was in middle school, and I was on the executive team of a large company. When the first Christmas holiday season rolled around, I was frenetically searching for the perfect gifts to send to my peers, working long hours, trying to attend every school celebration, and struggling to be an attentive spouse and conscientious caregiver to my elderly mother. At first, I couldn't understand why my male colleagues seemed to be rolling through the season without any signs of extra stress. It soon became clear that each one had a wife who was handling the list of holiday "to dos," which allowed them to remain focused on their jobs.

One study of high-achieving women in 2004 found that in two-thirds of cases where women choose to leave their careers, spouses were largely or partially a factor in the decision. In most cases, women quit to fill a parenting gap that their spouses were unwilling to fill.[19] A similar trend has been reported during the pandemic. In 2021, McKinsey & Company found that one in four women versus one in five men were considering leaving the workforce or downshifting their careers due to the pandemic. Most notably, the same study found that women with young children were nearly twice as likely as their male counterparts to be considering abandoning their careers altogether.[20] Of course, not all women with unsupportive spouses downscale or quit their jobs. Some choose to continue pursuing their leadership aspirations. Among those who do, however, upward mobility seems to come at a cost, often the cost of a spouse. By one estimate, approximately 60 percent of late-life divorces are initiated by women, in many cases because these women are eager to finally focus on their careers, which tend to gain momentum later in life.[21] There is also evidence that the divorce may not always be by choice. One Swedish study found that women promoted to political leadership roles (mayor or parliamentarian) were nearly twice as likely to end up divorced. The same did not hold true for men who end up assuming executive-level roles at large organizations.[22]

If having an unsupportive spouse poses an obstacle for women, having a supportive spouse seems to have the opposite effect. Richard Zweigenhaft, a professor of psychology at Guilford College in North Carolina and the coauthor of *The New CEOs* (2011), asks, "How do you compete without a spouse? Basically, you can't." In his study, Zweigenhaft found that an overwhelming number of American CEOs of both genders were married and had been for many years.[23] What neither Zweigenhaft's study nor any other studies I have read reveal is how many female CEOs have spouses who have downscaled their careers. If these data aren't readily available, it may simply reflect the fact that women in heterosexual relationships are often reluctant to draw attention to the sacrifices their spouses are making to support their professions because doing so may diminish their spouse's own successes. What is clear is that for both women and men, it isn't enough to have a spouse—they also need to have a conscientious spouse or one who is aware of the difficulties they face in a leadership position and is willing to pitch in. One Australian study found that having a conscientious spouse positively impacts employee income, promotions, and job satisfaction.[24]

While a supportive spouse appears to be important for women leaders, women looking for their own Doug Emhoff may find the search to be more challenging than expected. A study by Robert Mare at the University of California, Los Angeles, in 2016 found that although "assortative mating" (i.e., the coupling up of individuals with a similar level of education) is on the rise, there is little evidence that women coupling up with peers is leading to more power couples.[25] In other words, finding a spouse who is both an equal— someone who has similar career expectations and aspirations—and willing to step out of the spotlight seems to be ideal but not necessarily easily achievable for many women.

Fortunately for women, spouses aren't the only potential source of support. Many of the women I interviewed for this book also spoke of other private support channels that extended to family members and friends. In fact, some research suggests that compared to men's networks, women's relationships, particularly with other female peers, are generally stickier, "growing stronger, more mutual, and more interwoven over time."[26] Although this great stickiness can occasionally be a deficit (i.e., if and when a sticky relationship prevents one from expanding one's network or from moving on from a relationship that is no longer serving one), in most cases these personal networks are a clear advantage.

In my case, I can't imagine having a robust career without the laughter, shared storytelling, and regular meet-ups with treasured friends. For most women, friendships nurture their spirit and play a crucial role in their overall well-being. For some women, friends are especially important. Mirtha Villereal-Younger, the CEO of a construction company and former member of the military, talked to me about her "tribe" of women, describing them as a great gift. Alma Burke, a senior law enforcement leader, told me she looks to other women in her profession as an important source of validation. In her word, friends, especially those in law enforcement, "have empowered me to lead a life of truth and purpose." Several of the women I interviewed also discussed attempts to create sustainable informal networks in the workplace. For example, Hiltrud Werner, an executive at Volkswagen International, talked proudly about a program her company launched that involves members of the C-suite coming together with women across the organization. In this case, the informal conversations that take place on Zoom enable women outside the C-suite to ask questions of her and other executives, forge relationships across the organization's formal boundaries, and get facetime with top executives that they may otherwise not be able to secure.

Self-Reliance

A final channel of support is oneself. Given how isolated many women leaders become as they move up the ladder, knowing how to support and champion oneself isn't just a nice-to-have; it is a must-have for women leaders.

Andromachi Athanasopoulou and her colleagues suggest that one of the most critical factors in any woman leader's success is her ability to own her ambition. "This starts," they emphasize, "with seeing herself as a leader, which is by no means as simple as it sounds . . . because even once a woman has accepted her leadership potential, she may find it difficult to access formal development programs— either through lack of sponsorship or reluctance to self-promote." Athanasopoulou and her colleagues also identify four other factors that seem to help women rise to the top: acting without being asked to act, taking charge of one's personal and professional life, focusing on long-term goals, and embracing a well-rounded leadership style. These authors maintain, however, that women may be their own best channel of support because, by and large, "female leaders expect little outside support, either at home or in work."[27] But if a woman leader is often largely on her own, what is the best way to support herself?

What most women seek is solitude that can surface from even small moments in a day of chaos. The antidotes for an overdemanded life are usually found in the most obvious corners of our lives, and they are different for every woman. For some, the antidote is climbing into bed with a good book or taking a warm bath at the end of the day. For others, it might be taking a short walk or run, attending a Zumba or yoga class, or spending a morning in a church or temple. Of course, finding time to do this also seems to be a consistent problem for women. In *I Know How She Does It*, Laura Vanderkam reports that in dual-income households with children, men typically report having 4.5 hours more leisure time than their wives.[28] Although this amount of extra time may seem small, consider how long it might take to squeeze in a few yoga classes each week. In fact, that 4.5 hours of additional leisure time reported by men in dual-income households can be the difference between finding and not being able to find at least some time to oneself.

Building a robust ecosystem of support is critical for women leaders for both external and internal factors. As discussed at the start of this chapter, even in the 2020s women are still frequently excluded from networking opportunities. Formal and informal mentoring opportunities, coaching programs, and other channels of support can and do help compensate for women's ongoing exclusion from male-dominated networks. But this isn't the only reason it is critical for women to build a strong ecosystem of support. A robust ecosystem of support may also be able to help women counter another problem: feelings of self-doubt.

In a longitudinal survey of 360 reviews, the leadership consultants Jack Zenger and Joseph Folkman found that women score higher than men on 17 out of 19 capabilities that differentiate excellent leaders from average or poor leaders. Yet despite scoring higher than men in nearly all leadership categories, women often still fail to recognize their own strengths. As Zenger and Folkman further note, women's and men's levels of self-doubt also seem to vary across the life span. As they discovered, "At age 40, the confidence ratings [for women and men] merge. As people age, their confidence generally increases; surprisingly, over the age of 60, we see male confidence decline while female confidence increases. According to our data, men gain just 8.5 percentile points in confidence from age 25 to 60+ years. Women, on the other hand, gain 29 percentile points."[29] If Zenger and Folkman's findings are correct, then there is reason to conclude that women may be especially well served not only by establishing a complex ecosystem of support but also by establishing such an ecosystem early in their careers. On this account, organizations can make a notable difference.

It is tremendously difficult for any organization to change its culture, in part because fraternal networks often continue to thrive outside and on the borders of the organization. Rather than focus on dismantling long-standing fraternal networks that leave women on the sidelines, organizations are advised to focus on helping women build a supportive ecosystem and to do so from the start of their career when their confidence levels and ability to champion themselves may be most at risk. Here, it is important to recognize that building an ecosystem of support for women should involve not only developing mentorship programs but also changing the material conditions under which women experience their working lives.

Take, for example, the sportswear manufacturer Patagonia. The company was one of the first private companies in the United States to offer on-site childcare to employees. In 2017, under the leadership of the company's former CEO Rose Marcario, 100 percent of the company's female employees returned to work after giving birth.[30] The Patagonia example is notable for a simple reason. Much of the existing research and literature on how to support women's leadership focuses on fostering women's leadership qualities. If women aren't present in the workplace, however, such efforts are unlikely to yield very promising results. After all, for women to become a notable presence at the top echelons of any organization, a critical mass of women must be present across the ranks. Changing the material conditions of the workplace (e.g., offering affordable or free on-site childcare) is a concrete way any organization can begin to build a true ecosystem of support for women employees.

6

Succession Planning and Legacies

When Anne Mulcahy, former CEO of Xerox, stepped down from her post in 2009, she handed the company over to Ursula Burns—in the process, history was made on two accounts. Burns, who had started her career at Xerox as a summer intern back in 1980, became the first Black woman to lead a Fortune 500 company. She also became the first woman to ever succeed another woman CEO of a Fortune 500 company. There was nothing coincidental about this groundbreaking succession. It had been nearly a decade in the making. It was also an exception to the rule. Usually, when women leaders step down, there is no obvious successor, and if there is one, it is nearly always a man, not another woman.

Attention is often paid to why women leaders should proactively build bench strength in their organizations and how to do this in a way that includes positioning other women for potential leadership roles. This chapter examines this important question and addresses other largely overlooked questions that arise when women leaders exit their leadership positions. It examines how women leaders across industries proactively secure legacies that extend well beyond succession. Finally, this chapter explores what women leaders do after they exit from top leadership roles and the importance of their continued work on boards, in higher education, and in their communities.

Succession Wins and Losses

According to Catalyst, as of April 2020 women had succeeded other women as the CEOs of Fortune 500 companies on only three occasions. As already noted, Burns succeeded Mulcahy and served as CEO of Xerox from 2009 to 2017. In 2012, Sheri McCoy assumed Andrea Jung's CEO position at Avon Products. And in 2017, Debra Crew succeeded Susan Cameron as CEO of Reynolds American.[1] Although the Mulcahy–Burns hand-off at Xerox was successful, the other successions faltered. Avon struggled under McCoy's leadership,[2] and Crew served as CEO of Reynolds American for only one year.[3]

One might assume that corporate women-to-women successions represent an outlier, but even in sectors with a much higher percentage of women leaders, few women leaders seem to pass on their positions to other women leaders. Consider the succession records of women leaders in higher education. Although women now occupy roughly one-third of university president positions, data suggest that a woman leading a college or university is no guarantee more women will follow. A survey of all the women who held and completed terms in top leadership roles (i.e., president or chancellor) at US institutions from 2000 and 2010 reveals that less than 20 percent handed off the reins of power to another woman once they stepped down.

It is important to note that in the case of higher education, the problem may be that it is not the norm to have succession plans. One study published in 2016 found that although more than half of university presidents planned to leave their position in five years or sooner, only 24 percent had a succession plan.[4] But there may also be another problem at work here. As Cristina González's study on succession planning in higher education found in 2010, all too often "there is a tendency to have token candidates and to view diversity as a one-time commitment: once some women and minority administrators have been hired, no more are sought."[5] Said another way, many organizations, including universities, continue to treat equity as a checkbox. Once they have managed to install one woman or minority man in a top leadership role, they revert to their established way of operating, even if diversity, equity, and inclusion programs are communicated as top strategic priorities.

The challenge, then, rests not on individuals (i.e., finding a suitable replacement) but on organizations (i.e., finding a way to permanently break and rebuild how succession planning is done). Unfortunately, although there is already plenty of research on how to recruit women to executive leadership roles and why efforts to do so often fail, there is virtually no research on how women leaders engage in succession planning. The reason is rather obvious. There are so few women executive leaders that carrying out a broad study on women and succession planning would prove challenging, if not impossible, in most industries. There is, however, considerable research on succession planning in general and a growing body of research on how and why we can use succession planning to promote women and other minorities. Before we explore some of the existing literature on succession, though, it is important first to clarify what it is and why it matters.

To begin, succession planning is not simply a form of replacement hiring. Succession planning is about building bench strength by identifying and then supporting potential future leaders. Studies on succession planning tend to emphasize several key principles or best practices, many of which are common sense. Best practices in succession nearly always emphasize the fact that successful succession planning takes time (years rather than months in most cases). Some organizations view succession as an ongoing process rather than an event—something that is always under way. Best practices in C-suite succession also require board input and involvement. Moreover, whereas some experts strongly advise searching internally for future leaders, others suggest it is better to look beyond the organization.[6] A final and somewhat contentious issue is whether succession should focus on just one or two potential leaders or on a group of high potentials who will ultimately be asked to fight their way to the top position. I once encountered the latter situation while coaching several division presidents of a large corporation. The then CEO had hired me because he wanted each member of his executive team to have an equal opportunity to compete alongside external candidates when he eventually stepped down. In this case, each internal executive had access to coaching for two years, which was deemed adequate time to shore up weaknesses and reinforce strengths. When well orchestrated and managed, this approach can provide a valuable developmental opportunity for each individual and the team itself. But not everyone agrees it is best to pit internal candidates against each other.

Some leaders, including Mulcahy, maintain that it is not a good idea to have multiple successors in the running. By contrast, at some organizations—for example, General Electric—it has long been assumed that pitting successors against each other is the best option.[7] Some analysts even put a number on how many successors should be in the running for an organization's top position. For example, Victoria Luby and Jane Edison Stevenson, who are advisers at Korn Ferry, suggest seven potential CEOs should be actively being prepared at any time and that these candidates should represent different generations of potential leaders.[8]

Stephanie Bradley Smith, the vice president and chief human resources officer for DePaul University, recommends that as part of their diversity and inclusion mandate organizations should engage in regular audits of succession plans, asking, among other questions, whether their bench charts reflect a diverse pool of talent.[9]

Bradley Smith is right to recommend that succession planning be linked to diversity and inclusion initiatives, but best intentions aren't enough. Succession planning, at least when it is focused on finding an internal leader, nearly always pivots on identifying and grooming high-potential employees. As discussed at length in chapter 2 of this book, however, overcoming the embedded biases in how high potentials are identified and then supported is by no means easy. Just as high-potential programs may need to be broken down and rebuilt before they can start to work for women and other minorities, it seems possible that many best practices in succession planning may need to be radically rethought or abandoned and replaced before they can consistently work for women and other future minority leaders.

Successful Succession Planning and the Obstacles

To appreciate what succession planning looks like when diversity is part of the plan, it is useful to return to the Mulcahy–Burns handoff at Xerox.

As Mulcahy discussed in an article published shortly after this historic succession took place in 2009, the transition at Xerox was a long time coming. Mulcahy had met Burns in 1991, a full decade before Mulcahy became the CEO of Xerox. At the time, Burns was serving as an assistant to a senior Xerox executive, and Mulcahy was leading human resources. From the first encounter, Mulcahy was struck by Burns's presence and potential: "In many meetings she was the most junior person present, and people in that role are expected to listen and be invisible. Not Ursula. She offered opinions. She challenged points of view. Among the senior team there was a sense of 'Who *is* this person?' She was just so vocal. But I liked her authenticity and directness, even if she was a little rough around the edges."[10] Over the next decade, Mulcahy as chief of staff and Burns as lead of the product-development team continued to get to know each other. At that time, Mulcahy didn't think she was necessarily looking at Xerox's future CEO, but she was optimistic about Burns's prospects at Xerox or elsewhere.

As is often the case with high potentials, Burns's future leadership of Xerox was not guaranteed. As she rose internally, recruiters started to knock on her door. Internal changes at Xerox were also giving Burns reason to question her loyalty to the company. To retain Burns, Paul Allaire, a former Xerox CEO and one of Burns's mentors, eventually intervened, persuading her to stay based on news that the company would soon introduce new management. Within a year, Mulcahy had assumed the role of CEO. As Mulcahy notes, succession was never an afterthought for her or the organization: "From the moment I stepped into the job, the board began discussing who might succeed me. At that point, in 2001, we focused on four candidates and were considering two scenarios. The first was: What if something unexpected happens tomorrow, and we need someone really experienced who can step in immediately? The second was: What if we had the luxury of developing someone naturally over a long period of time? Ursula fit the second scenario—she needed more time to develop."[11]

Over the next decade, Mulcahy prepared Burns for her future role, and Burns's memoir, *Where You Are Is Not Who You Are* (2021), suggests she was aware of Mulcahy's plans early on.[12] Mulcahy did this by putting Burns into new and important roles and expanding her responsibilities, making sure that Burns became increasingly visible to board members, and proactively helping Burns build a stronger executive presence, including the ability to maintain a poker face no matter what happened in meetings. She also developed her capabilities in leading and engaging her team. As Mulcahy notes, "A person like Ursula, who really hates to waste time, can be tempted to cut through the crap and reach a conclusion that seems obvious to her. But it's important to realize that if, as CEO, you make your call too early, your team won't feel that it owns the outcome."[13] In other words, Mulcahy didn't just ensure that Burns was getting the experience and exposure she needed to eventually rise to the top but that she was also getting the skills needed to succeed when she did finally assume the role of CEO.

When it comes to succession, Mulcahy's advice to other leaders and organizations is clear: if you want to execute a succession plan, especially one that breaks new barriers, you need to plan far ahead. Indeed, she suggests that "the succession conversation between chief executives and their Boards needs to start a lot earlier than might feel comfortable. . . . [S]uccession should play out over three to five years at a minimum."[14]

Mulcahy demonstrated how a carefully conceived succession plan can have an impact, even resulting in a historic leadership breakthrough. Unfortunately, in many cases, placing the onus on women leaders to ensure they have not only a succession plan but also one that has been developed with an eye to promoting diversity may be too much to ask. This largely reflects the fact that the conditions under which women assume leadership roles often make it difficult or impossible for them to focus on succession concerns.

Succession Planning Needs Organizational Support
Succession planning may be driven by executives, but it can happen only with organizational buy-in. If you lead in a culture where succession planning has historically received little or no attention, turning your attention to succession planning as a leader may be viewed as a negative (e.g., something that is taking you away from more urgent or important matters). Often already under more scrutiny than their male counterparts, women leaders may face even greater scrutiny for investing time and energy in succession planning, especially early in their terms. As a result, depending on the

culture of the organization, building support for a diversity-focused succession plan may need to start by building awareness about the necessity for succession planning.

Perceived Bias

A second obstacle frequently faced by women leaders who seek to implement a succession plan focused on diversity is that women leaders are more likely than their male counterparts to be critiqued for driving what is perceived to be a personally motivated agenda. Historically, some women leaders appear to have taken extreme measures to avoid such accusations; for example, during her long-standing term as the prime minister of the United Kingdom Margaret Thatcher notoriously never appointed a single woman cabinet minister. Although Thatcher certainly represents an extreme, she isn't a complete outlier.

Women leaders, especially in male-dominated fields (e.g., law enforcement, the military, and engineering), are frequently under immense pressure to lead from a seemingly neutral position—one that is focused solely on excellence with no attention at all to concerns that may be perceived as personal or political. This may also explain why so few of the women I interviewed for this book spoke directly about succession planning and why most, when directly asked, had few insights on the process.

Succession Planning on the Glass Cliff

A final and significant challenge for women leaders is that they are all too often brought in to lead organizations that are already in crisis. When an organization is in crisis, succession planning typically gives way to a nearly singular focus on getting through and past that immediate crisis. Worse yet, women who end up leading in a glass-cliff situation frequently are brought in for short periods of time (sometimes less than a year) and then let go once they have cleaned up the mess left behind by their predecessor.

This was the case for a highly successful woman I interviewed for this book. A well-respected physician and scholar, she was asked to lead a medical school at a public research university after an executive leader had been removed due to a drug and sex scandal and then his successor, an interim leader, was also removed due to revelations about an earlier sexual harassment scandal. During her time leading the school, she not only addressed the fallout of her predecessors' scandals but also worked to renew the school's reputation and culture. With a focus on promoting diversity, equity, and inclusion—notably, before DEI initiatives went mainstream—she achieved a list of notable accomplishments during her tenure. However, before developing a complete succession plan, she was "nicely" asked if she was ready to go back to her faculty position. She had no say in her successor because, as far as the university and school were concerned, she had done her job well, and now the time was ripe to bring in a successor—a man, of course.

Beyond Succession—Leaving a Legacy

Although succession is important, many leaders leave a legacy through the work they carry out next. A survey of women who have led Fortune 500 companies reveals that stepping down rarely represents the end of their career and often simply represents the beginning of another important chapter in it. A small number of women executives move from leading one publicly traded company to another (e.g., Margaret Whitman transitioned from eBay to Hewlett Packard and eventually to General Motors). Others pivot to lead emerging companies (e.g., when Eileen Kullman left Dupont, she assumed the CEO position at Carbon—a digital manufacturing company founded in 2013). Still others assume entirely different ventures (e.g., when Andrea Jung stepped down from Avon after 13 years, she became CEO of Grameer America, a 501(c)3 nonprofit that offers loans and financial education to women living in poverty who want to start their own business). Not surprisingly, a significant number of former CEOs of Fortune 500 companies go on to serve as board members for other organizations, some at publicly held companies, others at regional health-care systems, universities, or nonprofits. In addition, some leaders move on to assume executive-level roles at other companies (e.g., when Laura Sen completed her term as CEO of BJ's Wholesale, she became the director of MassMutual).

Among the small sample of women who have led Fortune 500 companies, radical career pivots and retirement appear to be the least common postleadership moves. Only a small percentage of women CEOs drop out of public life after stepping down from their leadership roles (and most who do cite a personal or health-related reason). To date, only one former woman CEO of a Fortune 500 company has attempted a radical career pivot. Carly Fiorina attempted but failed to carve out a career in politics after being forced to resign from Hewlett Packard in 2005. First, Fiorina unsuccessfully ran for the US Senate in 2010. In 2016, she unsuccessfully ran as a Republican presidential nominee and later briefly served as Ted Cruz's announced running mate, but only for seven days. Despite failing to secure an elected position, Fiorina has served as a political adviser to Republican elected officials. But, overall, her attempt to engage in a major career pivot—from corporate leadership to politics—seems to be an exception to the rule.

Although I did not focus on succession issues in my interviews and very few interviewees raised these issues, I did ask research participants about the legacies they hoped to leave behind once they stepped out of their formal leadership positions. Here, it is worth noting that most of the women I spoke to did not aspire to subsequent public roles. In many cases, their responses were first and foremost personal.

Fiona Ma, California's state treasurer, spoke of her long-standing commitment to making a difference in underserved and underprivileged communities. As Ellen Stofan, under secretary for science and research at the Smithsonian and former NASA chief scientist, told me, "I do this work because it's important for me to move the needle in the STEM world so eventually the STEM world will look like the world itself. That is the legacy I'm invested in leaving behind." One of the military leaders I interviewed (who wasn't comfortable having her name used in this book) spoke of her legacy in more personal terms: "My legacy is to leave an impact on my nieces, cousins, and other family members, so they know that they don't have to start where I started. I want to have a long-lasting impact on my family, so they are already at the starting line, not far behind it like I was." When I asked Hiltrud Werner, an executive at Volkswagen, she paused and then said, "When I think about my legacy, I ask myself, What would I want to tell my daughter and son about my time in the organization?" Other women I interviewed spoke of their legacies through the lens of mentorship or as an opportunity to create structural changes that will make it possible for girls and women to be heard and thrive in the workplaces of tomorrow.

7

Roundtable on the Future of Women's Leadership

Even as I concluded writing this book, a set of urgent questions remained concerning the future of leadership for women in the twenty-first century. To further explore these questions and concerns, I asked four women leaders to come together to discuss what the future holds for women in leadership. To ensure that a range of perspectives would be represented, I reached out to women in several key sectors discussed throughout the book: Laura Mosqueda, a physician, educator, and the former dean of the Keck School of Medicine at the University of Southern California; Fiona Ma, a politician and California's state treasurer; Chief RaShall Brackney, a veteran law enforcement professional and the former chief of police for Charlottesville, Virginia; and Yasmin Beers, a management consultant and the former city manager of Glendale, California. Collectively, the women in the roundtable have experience working in the private sector, health care, higher education, local and state government, and law enforcement. They also all happen to belong to one or more racial and ethnic minorities. Since millennials (individuals born between the early 1980s and the mid-1990s) and Generation Z (individuals born between the mid-1990s and early 2010s) are the most racially and ethnically diverse generations ever to enter the workforce, it felt particularly important to assemble a group of women leaders who were able to speak professionally and personally to the interacting issues of gender, race, and ethnicity.

Carol Geffner: If you were sitting with a member of Gen Z who is just entering the workforce, what would you want to tell them? What should they be thinking about if they want to eventually move into leadership roles?

Laura Mosqueda: Don't take things personally. You have to understand that if someone acts out, it's not about you. You also have to be true to yourself—to know who you are and where your true north is. There will always be external demands and pressures that can knock you off your center, so it is crucial to remain true to your values. You also can't separate your personal and professional life. I have put a lot of effort into my growth, spirituality, and meditation. All of this helps me be a better person and a better professional.

Fiona Ma: Be a voice for those who don't have a voice, stand up, even if you're the only one standing up, and always remember who brought you to the dance. Let me give you an example of this final point.

Recently, there was a race for a position in the California Democratic Party. I was asked to support a millennial—a young Asian woman. There weren't any other Asians on the ticket, and I told her mentor that I would support her. Later, I was asked to support her again for another position on the [California Democratic Party] board. It became contentious when the comptroller stepped into the race, but I was already supporting this young activist, and I think we need to be doing this. Then, the week before the election the millennial tried to remove her mentor—who had helped her get this far—from the executive board during a meeting. The millennial, apparently after being pressured, argued that her mentor hadn't apologized to a group of victims who had come forward during a sexual harassment incident involving the board's former chair.

In the end, she didn't get the votes needed to remove her mentor, but it was still shocking. I withdrew my support and reminded the millennial, "You have to remember to be loyal to the people who got you here."

Ultimately, the millennial didn't win the election, and I don't know if she would have had she not tried to have her mentor removed from the board, but it's a good example of why you have to establish your values early and stick with them. I worry that young people don't always understand this. They will go with whatever they feel is going to potentially benefit them or what they are feeling in the moment. If you're always going to cave in to whatever or whoever is putting pressure on you, no one is going to have confidence in you. You're also not going to have any friends or allies because no one is going to trust you. That's a lesson for this new generation.

RaShall Brackney: I think when talking about leadership roles and younger millennials, they are still excited about being the first. They want to be the premier person in their field because, from the outside, it looks very glamorous. From the outside, if you look at a celebrity like Beyoncé, you just see someone who is at the pinnacle of her career. It's really the same in any field. But I would caution these younger women to start managing their expectations early on. As you move through whatever the ranks are in your profession, the succession planning and management tracks don't necessarily tell you everything about the journey. We see the glamour and excitement at the top, but we don't see the everyday struggles people went through to get to that point, and it's not glamorous. I may be called upon by Congress representatives and senators to be a subject-matter expert, and that may look really glamorous, but how did I get there? It didn't just happen. This was a 37-year journey, and it has been rough and rugged and tough. You need to manage your expectations. You need to know how long it will take you to get there and that it is not going to be as easy as the end product looks. My language and body language may be very composed now, but there are all these battle scars—every time you move up the ranks, you have to figure out a new way to manage.

Yasmin Beers: First and foremost, what I would say to anyone, particularly women, is to follow your dreams. Follow your dreams, and you can be and do anything you set your eyes on. That is what I say to my 13-year-old daughter, but I don't even really need to say that because I think innately she has somehow picked up on that. Once you do set your eyes on what that goal is, of course, there are going to be trials and tribulations, ups and downs, successes. You're going to have an array of emotions, feelings, and experiences, which will ultimately hopefully get you where you want to go, but it's important to remember that everyone's journey is different, and it is going to depend on the type of profession you choose. I've always been of the mindset that you need to prepare yourself well for whatever you want to achieve—maybe even prepare a bit more than your competitors, but without taking yourself too seriously. There has to be some levity and some humor and some ability to pivot if it doesn't work out, so you can still go for it again when the appropriate time comes.

Carol Geffner: It is one thing to say, "Follow your dreams," but what if you don't know where you're going next? Or what if you do know where you're going or think you're going, but you want it to happen immediately? How should we be preparing future women leaders for the journey ahead?

RaShall Brackney: You're right. By the time I was in my first chief position, I was 30 years into the profession. It's a good goal to have your eye on where you want to be at the end of all of this—that's laudable—but you better have a plan on how you're going to execute this. And there is no plan that I know of that gets you there on day one—unless you have an inheritance or endowment or it's your family business. But here is what I will also say: like anything else, if you're going after something in the field that you're passionate about, that it flies by—for me, it had been 37 years—but that time really does fly by. I know it's a cliché, but it's so true. Embedding yourself in whatever it is you're passionate about will allow you to be successful. You will then become the subject-matter expert that is recognized.

Fiona Ma: I would say that to this day you have to find a mentor or sponsor who will help you get where you want to go. It's very hard for women to make it on their own. There are always people who are going to be in your ear saying hire this person who is the daughter or son of so and so. Without that outside pressure, perhaps, we could look at a pool and hire very qualified people. But as it turns out, people tend to hire people they have something in common with—some previous relationship, people connection from another life or network. It's a reality. So you need to find a mentor or sponsor who is going to help you get where you want to go. You can work as much as you want. You can work 16-hour days, publish papers, get awards, but unless you have someone who is saying, "She deserves it, this is my pick," you're never going to get where you want to go.

Yasmin Beers: I knew early on, even in junior high school, that I was going to be involved with my community—perhaps engaged in nonprofit work—but I didn't know in what specific capacity. When I was 17, I signed up to become a library page. I was making $3 an hour. At that time, I wasn't thinking that I would one day become the city manager, but I knew in my heart of hearts I would always be doing something that involved giving back to a community. Maybe, when you do have a desire, you set yourself up to achieve it, so you're attracted to certain positions or jobs at a very young age that make sense to you. I also tried to work in a deli at one point, but it didn't speak to me in the way shelving books did at this small community library. The library had more meaning. As I went on, each new role at the library, combined with my education, helped me clarify my interest and what I wanted to do as my life's work. But it didn't happen overnight. I was at the library for 13 years. In the end, that part-time job that I started in high school gave me a lot of important insights. From an operational perspective, I came to understand how operations and how municipal governments in general work. I eventually applied for the deputy city manager position, but I was still young and very green, but I got the position because it was ultimately the right fit.

Carol Geffner: We're having this discussion as many people are looking back on the impact of the pandemic. It has been tough on all leaders, but a growing body of research suggests that women outperformed men as leaders during this crisis. Do you agree, and why do you think women have outperformed men over the past year?

Fiona Ma: I think women have more empathy and compassion than men, and we understand how difficult it is to be a mother, be a wife, be a caregiver, and when it comes to tough times, I think men are more likely to just lay everyone off for the bottom line. They have to make sure their stock prices stay up. They don't think long term for the most part. For women, it's different. They are thinking we need to keep as many people on the payroll as possible because they need it—they need the health care and the retirement accounts. Also, women know how difficult it is for women, when they lose their job, to get another high-paying quality job. So I think for women leaders it has been more important to make accommodations to keep everyone employed. I think women leaders also appreciated that keeping people around has a long-term impact because they could see when we get out of the pandemic, these employees are going to be loyal—they're going to band with us and work harder because we didn't lay them off.

RaShall Brackney: Women have outperformed men during the pandemic because this is our lived experience. I didn't have to imagine what working and doing childcare all day was going to be like because I've already experienced it. That's the benefit of the millennial employee having someone like me in this position. I know what it feels like to do shift work and to be due at work at 10:30 at night and to have a husband who won't be home from his shift until midnight and to have a two-year-old. I know what it's like to be wondering who is going to come over and babysit at your house for just two hours or at midnight? The answer is no one. It is really difficult. So with my staff here I have been extremely accommodating. I understand how tough it can be when you have time constraints, and you're trying to make a doctor's appointment and other obligations. So the reason women are now outperforming men is obvious—even before the pandemic, this was our lived experience. We already know what it is like to find yourself in a place where we're the primary caretakers of family—our children, spouses, and even parents and extended family. We understand the need for flexibility and support and the value of not having to worry about your income and health care and your profession and job at the same time. I suspect that police departments led by women, like businesses, are also outperforming for this reason.

Yasmin Beers: You know, some of my most fulfilling years in city government were when we were in crisis. I was also still there for the first six months of the pandemic, and I felt that the organization was in a good place. Even though we were in the pandemic, I felt that the organization was in a good place. I wouldn't have left if I had any doubt. I was very comfortable leading in that situation, and when I say comfortable, I am not saying that being in crisis isn't painful and doesn't cause sleepless nights. After I left, other local leaders like the fire chief told me I wouldn't have wanted to go through that with anyone else because of your ability to make decisions quickly but also with care and compassion. I don't know specifically why women leaders are doing well in this scenario, but, for me, I thrive under pressure, and this pandemic was one of those situations. In a week, our organization, with more than 1,500 full-time employees, went remote. We also kept providing all the same services and kept holding all meetings. With me, what you see is what you get. My team never has to wonder where I'm coming from, unless it's confidential, and that transparency has helped me lead during crises, including the pandemic. I'm also not afraid to make decisions and to say it's on me if it doesn't work out, so everyone knows that if something goes wrong, I have their backs, and I would never, never jeopardize their professional standing.

Carol Geffner: Are you optimistic about the future of women in leadership?

Laura Mosqueda: Yes, I see a lot of women helping other women. That's my experience, and that is having an impact. But at the organizational level I think a lot of DEI is all talk. Organizations say they are committed to DEI, but it's more about checking off boxes. People at the top don't really believe in it. Organizations are not incentivized to think long term—for example, 10 to 15 years out. Whether it's a private industry that has to respond to stakeholders or higher education, it doesn't matter. The decisions are so often focused on short-term metrics. In higher education, it's about rankings, getting grants, etc. The external metrics drive behavior. Another barrier we need to address in organizations is fear. White men who have held powerful positions are worried. This is understandable. And it can become very quietly nasty behind the scenes. So, building a culture where psychological safety supports future women leaders [is important].

Fiona Ma: There are certain women who are doing better, but on the whole I don't see this forward movement. When Meg Whitman was leading eBay and Marissa Mayer was Yahoo, we thought great—women are making inroads and are going to lead in tech, but, of course, that hasn't happened. Consider banking. Of all the major banks, we have one woman leading a major bank. I don't really see women en masse rising to these positions. If you look at the Forbes Top 100, how much has it changed over the past decade? There are still only a handful of women on that list. Who are the wealthiest women we can name? It's the exwife of Jeff Bezos and exwife of Bill Gates, so you see that it's the men who are continuing to accumulate the wealth. I'm not hopeful that this will change anytime soon. I recently met a billionaire—yes, a real billionaire—and he said, "What do you need?" I said, "I would like to meet more people," and immediately he said, "Have you met this person? I went to Harvard with him. Have you met this person? He's a member at my golf club. Have you met this person? We race together on the weekends." He immediately named six very wealthy men who are all part of the old boys' network. Women still don't have that. We still don't have billionaires that strategize on what they can do if they put their money together. When women get together, we're still talking about what good cause we can support. Think about this in terms of politics. There is still not a single woman who can fund a campaign herself. Women still don't have access to that type of wealth.

RaShall Brackney: There is optimism, and there is being hopeful. Optimism allows you to think about the possibilities, and hopeful seems to be a bit more localized. I'm less optimistic about movement across the nation and around the globe on these issues. I'm hopeful that there are little signs that we could, if we're willing and interested, move the needle, but I'm not convinced we have the appetite for it because I think there's a real risk that once you've had the first and only woman leader, many people think that's enough. We see this in politics. Now that we've had a Black president, we're a postracial society. Now that we have a female who is vice president, we no longer have gender issues. But every day we see how women are significantly underpaid for performing the exact same work. Because we don't have the networks to talk to each other about what our value or worth is in this space, we have no barometers to compare, so we're always going to be at a disadvantage unless we're relying on a male in a leadership position to help bring us along.

Yasmin Beers: I'm somewhat optimistic as more women do step into leadership roles. For example, I didn't realize how important it was for some of the females in my organization to see another female heading the organization. This was something that would come [up] every so often, whether it was in a casual conversation or in my office. Women would say to me, "You get it." I wondered, "What did I 'get' that my predecessor—who was really loved—didn't get?" He was also open and inclusive. But so many women have told me that I got it more. Specifically, a lot of women have told me that I just understand what it means to be balancing one's career with motherhood and that it's okay to be on maternity leave and not feel guilty, even though we know this is okay from a legal perspective. They also talked about other things—the nuances of how I spoke in meetings and how that impacted inclusion. I still don't totally understand what I was doing differently, but I think just being female represents something to many young, up-and-coming female professionals who can then see themselves in the same position and see that it is obtainable.

Carol Geffner: So, what do you tell young women who want to think big and imagine a future in leadership?

Laura Mosqueda: Have fun, stay playful, hold on to your curiosity, and have a sense of humor about yourself. All these things are so important. It's also important to pick your battles and let people know why because you can't solve everything. This all comes back to knowing your values and staying true to them. Finally, you need to be aware of how to use your position for good—to help others. Leadership roles offer an opportunity to make a profound difference.

RaShall Brackney: Within the policing profession, there were jobs I absolutely despised, but what kept me going was asking myself, "Is there something I can take out of this job that will help me continue my professional development?" There is something in that position—the good, bad, and the ugly that will enable you to be successful. Every position has the potential to give you some ability or skill or some form of knowledge that your counterparts—those people you're in competition with—don't have. This can bring you a more nuanced set of skills. Someone who is only willing to do what they are passionate about is not necessarily the person who will eventually make the best leader.

You also have to keep learning. The first time I was told I had to take a budget class, I was so upset. I didn't have any idea about things like profit-and-loss statements and depreciation values and actuals versus spending. But now as we're talking about defunding the police, I have a comfort level talking about this issue. I can speak with authority about the service-industry models we have and the funding models we're going to need to support that and about the impact on services if I don't have those resources.

Fiona Ma: Networking is also important. Make sure you're networking with the right people. You only have so many hours in the week. Are you still only having drinks with your friends? That's great, but they might not be the people who are going to help you get ahead in life necessarily. You need to put an effort into getting out of your comfort zone. If you're not invited, you may have to ask people to have dinner or drinks or lunch, and that can be intimidating, but it's important. Also, know your audience. You have to understand people and what motivates them. When I'm trying to put together a team, I have to remember that the people I like best aren't always the best people for a job. You have to understand where people are coming from and put them in a place where they can succeed.

Yasmin Beers: My advice is to focus on relationships. The relationships you build will carry you through the good and the bad times, even crises. I would also say that each position you step into will bring teachable moments. All your education and your volunteer work—for example, holding board positions on nonprofits—will also bring teachable moments. Finally, I would say, don't take yourself so seriously until you have to. This isn't to say that there aren't times when you'll have to show your teeth and set the record straight. I've had to do that a couple of times in my career, and it turned out fine because I have always known my boundaries. If your boundaries are clear to yourself, there is no question as to what those boundaries should be with others, so clarifying your boundaries early on is also essential.

Carol Geffner: And what do you want to tell organizations and their leaders? What do they need to be doing to bring about system-level change?

Laura Mosqueda: I work in academia, which is a very unique system, but it is also an archaic system that no longer functions well. Worse yet, we have a death grip on how things currently work, and the people in positions of power want to maintain the status quo because it has worked well for them. But when I look at junior and midlevel faculty, I honestly don't think the current tenure system works well for them at all. I think the entire system needs to be blown up and looked at with completely fresh eyes for the twenty-first century. The current structures need to be destroyed and redesigned.

Another obstacle is the pressure to be number one, which is always weighing on you as a medical school. It's hard to have a long-term vision when you're thinking about next year's NIH [National Institutes of Health] ranking. So what's the answer? I personally think you have to stop thinking about your ranking for a few years, and I really do believe if you do the right thing, you will see change. But it takes time for that to evolve. You have to have deeply held values committed to diversity and equity to say you're willing to invest for the long term.

RaShall Brackney: When you think about what an organization can do, I don't see any clear strategic plans, even at the level of the federal government, which is one of our largest employers. If we had systems already working that we could put in place, we could more easily change and influence the narrative about women in leadership roles.

I am always thinking about how we might do things differently and what would have benefited me had I known what the insiders knew before I entered my system. What would it have been like if I had come into policing knowing what the people who built the systems know about the systems, the back doors, the side doors, and the ways you get into the office? When you design systems, you know every hidden back door, you know every way to access those systems to your advantage, but you also know every way in which you can shut down and eliminate opportunities for somebody you don't want to be part of your system. This is what needs to change.

Conclusion: Five Pillars of Change

I initiated this book in 2019 when I began to carry out a series of interviews with women leaders. At the time, the future seemed bright, or at least brighter than it had in the past, as more women than ever before were rising into leadership roles. Since I started working on this book, the world has changed in ways I couldn't have predicted in 2019. Some of these changes may ultimately prove groundbreaking for women and other minorities pursuing leadership positions, whereas others may represent a huge setback.

First, in the wake of the powerful protests that followed the death of George Floyd in the spring of 2020, many organizations that had never before seriously thought about diversity, equity, and inclusion started to reflect upon their organizations, C-suites, and organizational cultures. By late summer of 2020, thousands of organizations across the United States and worldwide had published statements outlining their approach to DEI, and a growing number of leaders had begun to come forward to share thought leadership on the topic. Whether this self-reflective moment will be sustained over time or have an impact on who ends up leading organizations now and in the future is yet to be seen. Either way, I would be remiss to ignore that this was one of the first times in my working life that I have witnessed so many organizations and leaders seriously addressing DEI issues. At the same time, however, something else was happening.

After years of slow and steady progress, we witnessed a massive exit of women from the workforce during the pandemic and an equally notable trend of women downscaling their ambitions (e.g., stepping out of demanding leadership roles). The major challenge facing these women was the increased demands on their time on the home front as remote work combined with remote schooling found many working mothers doing double duty throughout the workday. As early as September 2020, troubling reports started to appear about the pandemic's impact on women's current employment participation and about its long-term impact on gender diversity in the leadership pipeline.

In the fall of 2020, a McKinsey & Company study reported that as many as two million women were considering leaving the workforce due to the COVID-19 pandemic.[1] Subsequent studies revealed that women were not just thinking about leaving the workforce but were already doing so or being pushed out due to layoffs. Between November 2020 and January 2021, IBM surveyed more than 2,600 executives, middle managers, and professional women and men working in the same 10 industries and 9 geographic regions that it had previously surveyed in 2019. The study's findings revealed a troubling trend that appeared to have been exacerbated by the pandemic: a notable drop in women in senior vice president, vice president, director, and manager roles. The IBM study also warned, "This contraction aligns with other dire statistics showing that women in the early and middle stages of their careers are most vulnerable to pandemic-related job displacements, with those aged 20 to 34 among the hardest hit."[2] The "dire statistics" to which the IBM study was referring included a finding by the National Women's Law Center in February 2021 that 2.3 percent of women had left the labor force in the United States between February 2020 and January

2021, bringing women's labor participation back down to levels not seen since 1988.[3] Notably, around the same time other global studies suggested the US labor trend was not an outlier. One Canadian study, for example, found that women were 10 times more likely than men to have permanently exited the workforce during the pandemic.[4]

Although the actual fallout of the pandemic on women's labor-force participation may take years to become fully visible in the United States and around the world, the grim statistics encountered during the pandemic revealed just how tenuous women's position in the workforce and leadership pipeline remains. In many respects, the pandemic reminded us that women are not just fighting to ascend into leadership roles. During challenging economic times, they may also still find themselves fighting to remain in the workforce at all. And, as in the past, women with young children (primarily women in their late twenties to midforties) seem to be most at risk.

Although I don't claim to have all the answers, over the course of researching and writing this book I have encountered five pillars that can help us in our struggle to build organizations that consistently work for women.

I   Set the Tone at the Top

Whether an organization is led by a CEO or by a president, chief, or general, it is important that the person at the top publicly commit to building diverse, equitable, and inclusive systems and that this individual be held accountable for achieving specific results. This means doing much more than stating that DEI is a priority or offering training programs or short-term initiatives simply to create the appearance of an organizational commitment to DEI. In large corporations as well as public institutions, this means allocating substantial resources to building a DEI ecosystem that will ultimately touch every level of the organization. To do this, leaders need to ensure that everyone from the board of directors to the C-suite to the human resources department has skin in the game. After all, in most organizations, building a DEI ecosystem that starts at the top and ripples across the organization requires large-scale buy-in. Everyone from the top down must be prepared to engage in deep learning about unconscious biases and how these biases are structuring their decision making. The only way to execute an organizational overhaul of this nature is to communicate a clear and consistent message from the top of the organization and an accountable execution plan.

II   Prepare for a System Overhaul

As discussed throughout this book, organizations don't fail women due to the presence of just a few bad apples. Biases don't just live in individuals. They also live in systems, which include an entire array of policies, structures, and practices. As a result, building organizations that work for women has to start with a comprehensive and systemic transformation. In most cases, this includes an overhaul of all human resource systems, processes, and practices (e.g., how an organization recruits and hires talent, carries out performance reviews, and connects measurable results to incentive compensation). Doing this work isn't easy. Most human resource systems at long-standing companies were developed when there were still few or no women or visible minorities in management-level roles. This is why just making tweaks to existing systems and processes will ultimately prove to be inadequate. As many of the women I interviewed for this book concluded, especially when pushed to offer concrete advice on how to address workplace inequities for women and other minorities in the twenty-first century, sometimes the best way forward is to start by abandoning current systems and designing new ones for the future.

III   Introduce Scorecards

We have all heard the adage, "What gets measured gets managed." This adage also holds true in the case of DEI. For example, consider the Human Rights Campaign's Corporate Equality Index, which measures how corporations' policies and practices support LGBTQ employees. The index doesn't dictate what policies corporations should adopt. It simply holds up a mirror to the state of one's workplace so a corporation can see where it stands, including how it stacks up in comparison to other organizations. In 2002, only 13 businesses received a 100 percent rating on the Corporate Equality Index. Within a decade, more than 300 businesses had reached this rating. But when it comes to DEI, corporations and other organizations should consider external benchmarks as only one reference point for measuring progress. These benchmarks must be accompanied by internal scorecards and evaluation processes to measure and promote DEI. For this approach to work, an organization's objectives and measurement need to be transparent (e.g., highlighted in prime locations inside the organization, on the company's websites, in annual reports, in shareholder reports, etc.). Progress at the unit, department, and division level should also be visible within the organization. And at every level, managers should be held accountable for communicating and implementing the action plans developed with their employees. Combined, these practices hold the potential to send a clear message that the organization is fully and publicly accountable for advancing DEI.

IV   Incentivize Progress

There also appears to be a compelling reason for organizations to start incentivizing DEI gains. Internally, this might mean offering clear rewards to each member of the C-suite, executives, units, departments, or divisions that achieve their objectives and make progress on DEI (e.g., overhauling hiring or promotion practices and demonstrating clear results). If there is any doubt that this approach can work, consider what happened after the passage of the Affordable Care Act in 2010: the US health-care delivery system was forced to change its fundamental business model because reimbursement of funds from the government became tied to patient-satisfaction results. This meant that hospitals had to quickly discover how to put patient needs at the center of care, which shockingly was something many hospitals hadn't prioritized in the past. Now imagine what would happen if organizations or individual units, departments, or divisions within organizations had clear financial incentives (e.g., additional hiring lines, larger annual budgets, or bonus compensation) for making measurable progress on DEI priorities? Like it or not, rewarding individuals and teams for making measurable progress on DEI priorities (e.g., offering teams that diversify access to additional hiring lines) communicates the importance of this strategic priority and adds a sense of urgency to accelerate the pace of change.

V   Support Employees and Their Families

Finally, and perhaps most urgently, organizations committed to advancing the rise of women leaders need to take a deep look at their employees' needs and to implement strategies that will make a noticeable difference in supporting women and their families. For example, we know that women are often knocked off course mid-career due to the demands of raising a family. There is also evidence that introducing affordable or free onsite childcare (or subsidizing offsite childcare) can radically reduce attrition rates. Even if a national childcare program may be the best solution, while politicians continue to debate the cost and merits of such an initiative, organizations can step in to fill the gap. Once again, as the surge of women from the workforce during the pandemic demonstrated, women aren't just fighting to rise up the ranks but in some cases simply to hang on to the positions they currently occupy. Structural support, which includes access to affordable and quality childcare, may ultimately prove to be the very best investment an organization can make when it comes to supporting women at all stages of the career cycle.

Admittedly, some of the pillars outlined in this chapter will take time to execute, but others can be immediately embraced and put into practice. Ultimately, the onus rests on boards of directors, the C-suite, and organizational leaders to take up the call to level-up their commitment to DEI and start building organizations that work for, rather than against, women. If enough leaders respond to this call, I'm confident that the C-suites and boards of the future may finally begin to reflect the diversity found in the entry-level ranks of nearly all professions in the twenty-first century.

Notes

Chapter 1

1. Korn Ferry, "No Room at the Top," survey, May 23, 2019, https://www.kornferry .com/about-us/press/no-room-at-the-top.

2. Catalyst, "Historical List of Women CEOs of the Fortune Lists: 1972–2020," June 2019, https://www.catalyst.org/wp-content/uploads/2019/06/Catalyst_Women_Fortune _CEOs_1972-2020_Historical_List_5.28.2020.pdf.

3. Catherine H. Tinsley and Kate Purmal, "Research: Board Experience Is Helping More Women Get CEO Jobs," *Harvard Business Review*, July 29, 2019, https://hbr .org/2019/07/research-Board-experience-is-helping-more-women-get-ceo-jobs. As Tinsley and Purmal report, "More than half of the women (59%) served on a public company Board, as compared with 42% of the men. Almost twice as many women (23%) as men (12%) served on a private company Board."

4. Nora Bensahel, David Barno, Katherine Kidder, and Kelley Sayler, *Battlefields and Boardrooms: Women's Leadership in the Military and the Private Sector* (Washington, DC: Center for a New American Security, January 2015), https://www.files.ethz.ch /isn/187251/CNAS_BattlefieldsVsBoardrooms_BensahelBarnoKidderSayler.pdf.

5. Council for Foreign Relations, "Demographics of the U.S. Military," July 13, 2020, https://www.cfr.org/backgrounder/demographics-us-military.

6. Shelley S. Hyland and Elizabeth Davis, *Local Police Departments, 2016: Personnel* (Washington, DC: US Department of Justice, Bureau of Justice Statistics, 2016), https://www.bjs.gov/content/pub/pdf/lpd16p.pdf.

7. Dorothy Schulz, "Why Are America's Women Police Chiefs Resigning?," *Crime Report*, August 13, 2020, https://thecrimereport.org/2020/08/13/why-are-americas -women-police-chiefs-resigning/.

8. David B. Muhlhausen, *Women in Policing: Breaking Barriers and Blazing a Path* (Washington, DC: National Institute of Justice, 2019), https://www.ncjrs.gov/pdf files1/nij/252963.pdf.

9. Ellie Bothwell, "Female Leadership in Top Universities Advances for First Time since 2017," *Times Higher Education Supplement*, March 6, 2020, https://www .timeshighereducation.com/news/female-leadership-top-universities-advances -first-time-2017.

10. KPMG, *Women's Leadership Study* (London: KPMG, 2014), https://assets.kpmg /content/dam/kpmg/ph/pdf/ThoughtLeadershipPublications/KPMGWomensLeader shipStudy.pdf.

11. See, among other studies, Deloitte, *Women in the Board Room: A Global Perspective*, 6th ed. (London: Deloitte, 2019), https://www2.deloitte.com/content/dam /Deloitte/global/Documents/Risk/gx-risk-women-in-the-Boardroom-sixth-edition .pdf.

12. Jane Stevenson and Dan Kaplan, "Women C-Suite Ranks Nudge Up—a Tad," Korn Ferry, 2019, https://www.kornferry.com/insights/articles/women-in-leader ship-2019-statistics.

13. Judith Warner and Danielle Corley, "The Women's Leadership Gap," Center for American Progress, November 20, 2018, https://www.americanprogress.org/issues /women/reports/2018/11/20/461273/womens-leadership-gap-2/.

14. William Scarborough, "What the Data Says about Women in Management between 1980 and 2010," *Harvard Business Review*, February 23, 2018, https://hbr .org/2018/02/what-the-data-says-about-women-in-management-between-1980-and -2010?registration=success.

15. Stephen Miller, "CHRO Pay Trails Other Top Executives," SHRM, October 3, 2016, https://www.shrm.org/resourcesandtools/hr-topics/compensation/pages/chro -pay-trails.aspx.

16. Scarborough, "What the Data Says about Women in Management between 1980 and 2010."

17. Mariela V. Campuzano, "Force and Inertia: A Systematic Review of Women's Leadership in Male-Dominated Organizational Cultures in the United States," *Human Resource Development Review* 18, no. 4 (2019): 437–469, https://doi.org/10 .1177/1534484319861169.

18. Melissa Fisher, "Wall Street Women: Professional Saviors of the Global Economy," *Critical Perspectives on International Business* 11 (2015): 137–155.

19. American Council on Education, *American College President Study* (Washington, DC: American Council on Education, 2017), https://www.aceacps.org/women-presi dents/#demographics.

20. Bridget Turner Kelly, "Though More Women Are on College Campuses, Climbing the Professor Ladder Remains a Challenge," Brookings Institution, March 29, 2019, https://www.brookings.edu/blog/brown-center-chalkBoard/2019/03/29/though -more-women-are-on-college-campuses-climbing-the-professor-ladder-remains-a -challenge/#:~:text=Women%20made%20up%2031%20percent,has%20tripled%20 during%20this%20period.

21. Ioana M. Latu, Marianne Schmid Mast, Dario Bombari, Joris Lammers, and Crystal L. Hoyt, "Empowering Mimicry: Female Leader Role Models Empower Women in Leadership Tasks through Body Posture Mimicry," *Sex Roles* 80, no. 1 (2019): 11–24, https://doi.org/10.1007/s11199-018-0911-y.

22. Sheryl Sandberg, *Lean In: Women, Work, and the Will to Lead* (New York: Knopf, 2013), 10.

23. Judith Newman, "'Lean In': Five Years Later," *New York Times*, March 16, 2018, https://www.nytimes.com/2018/03/16/business/lean-in-five-years-later.html#: ~:text=It%20rode%20the%20New%20York,all%20formats)%2C%20landed%20Ms.

24. Sandberg, *Lean In*, 10.

25. Zoe Williams, "*Lean In: Women, Work, and the Will to Lead* by Sheryl Sandberg—Review," *Guardian*, March 13, 2013, https://www.theguardian.com/books/2013/mar /13/lean-in-sheryl-sandberg-review.

26. bell hooks, "Dig Deep: Beyond Lean In," *Feminist Wire*, October 28, 2013, https://thefeministwire.com/2013/10/17973/.

27. Jessica Stillman, "Michelle Obama Just Said 'Lean In' Doesn't Work. Here's the Study That Proves She's Right," *Inc.*, December 7, 2018, https://www.inc.com /jessica-stillman/michelle-obama-is-really-not-a-fan-of-sheryl-sandbergs-lean-in.html.

28. Kimberly Weisul, "How Playing the Long Game Made Elizabeth Holmes a Billionaire," *Inc.*, October 2015, https://www.inc.com/magazine/201510/kimberly-wei sul/the-longest-game.html.

29. Henry A. Kissinger, "Elizabeth Holmes," *Time*, April 16, 2015, https://time.com /collection-post/3822734/elizabeth-holmes-2015-time-100/.

30. John Carreyrou, "Hot Startup Theranos Has Struggled With Its Blood-Test Technology," *Wall Street Journal*, last updated October 16, 2015, https://www.wsj.com /articles/theranos-has-struggled-with-blood-tests-1444881901.

31. Michal Lev-Ram, "Theranos' Elizabeth Holmes Calls on Women to Help Each Other," *Fortune*, October 12, 2015, https://fortune.com/2015/10/12/elizabeth-holmes -calls-on-women/.

32. Kate Clark, "US VC Investment in Female Founders Hits All-Time High," *Tech-Crunch*, December 9, 2019, https://techcrunch.com/2019/12/09/us-vc-investment -in-female-founders-hits-all-time-high/.

33. Susan Fowler, "Reflecting on One Very, Very Strange Year at Uber," *SusanFowler .com* (blog), February 19, 2017, https://www.susanjfowler.com/blog/2017/2/19/ref lecting-on-one-very-strange-year-at-uber.

34. Reuters, "Uber's Revenue Hits $6.5 Billion in 2016, Still Has Large Loss," April 14, 2017, https://www.reuters.com/article/us-uber-tech-results/ubers-revenue-hits-6 -5-billion-in-2016-still-has-large-loss-idUSKBN17G1IB.

35. Trae Vassallo, Ellen Levy, Michele Madansky, Hillary Mickell, Bennett Porter, and Monica Leas, "Elephant in the Valley," survey, n.d., https://www.elephant inthevalley.com/.

36. Ian Hathaway, "The Ascent of Women-Led Venture-Backed Startups in the United States," Center for American Entrepreneurship, 2017, http://www.startupsusa .org/women-founded-venture-backed-startups/.

37. Campuzano, "Force and Inertia," 442.

38. Edgar Schein, *Organizational Culture and Leadership* (San Francisco: Jossey-Bass, 2010), 320–321.

Chapter 2

1. Cindy Pace, "How Women of Color Get to Senior Management," *Harvard Business Review*, August 31, 2018, https://hbr.org/2018/08/how-women-of-color-get-to -senior-management.

2. Francesca Gino, "The Business Case for Curiosity," *Harvard Business Review*, September–October 2018, https://hbr.org/2018/09/the-business-case-for-curiosity.

3. Michael Harvey, Milorad Novicevic, Nancy Leonard, and Dinah Payne, "The Role of Curiosity in Global Managers' Decision-Making," *Journal of Leadership & Organizational Studies* 13, no. 3 (2007): 43–58, https://doi.org/10.1177/107179190701300 30401.

4. David Bickett, Jochen Schweitzer, Emmanuel Mastio, "Curiosity in Leadership: A Strategic Paradox," paper presented at the European Group for Organizational Studies Conference, 2019, https://opus.lib.uts.edu.au/handle/10453/133969.

5. Notably, as Ruchika Tulshyan and Jodi-Ann Burey observe, although imposter syndrome may exist, the concept has also been used to misplace the blame for toxic workplace enviroments onto individuals. Recognizing that women and visible minorities are especially likely to feel doubt in the workplace, "leaders must create a culture for women and people of color that addresses systemic bias and racism. Only by doing so can we reduce the experiences that culminate in so-called impostor syndrome among employees from marginalized communities—or at the very least, help those employees channel healthy self-doubt into positive motivation, which is best fostered within a supportive work culture" ("Stop Telling Women They Have Imposter Syndrome," *Harvard Business Review*, February 11, 2021, https://hbr.org/2021/02/stop-telling-women-they-have-imposter-syndrome).

6. Merryn McKinnon and Christine O'Connell, "Perceptions of Stereotypes Applied to Women Who Publicly Communicate Their STEM Work," *Humanities and Social Science Communications* 7 (2020): article 160, https://doi.org/10.1057/s41599-020 -00654-0.

7. Natasha Quadlin, "The Mark of a Woman's Record: Gender and Academic Performance in Hiring," *American Sociological Review* 83, no. 2 (2018): 331–360, https://doi.org/10.1177/0003122418762291.

8. PwC, "Putting Purpose to Work: A Study of Purpose in the Workplace," June 2016, https://www.pwc.com/us/en/about-us/corporate-responsibility/assets/pwc -putting-purpose-to-work-purpose-survey-report.pdf.

9. Marlene G. Fine, "Women Leaders' Discursive Constructions of Leadership," *Women's Studies in Communication* 32, no. 2 (2009): 190.

10. Herminia Ibarra, Robin Ely, and Deborah Kolb, "Women Rising: The Unseen Barriers," *Harvard Business Review*, September 2013, http://dx.doi.org/10.2469/dig .v43.n5.1

11. Vanessa Burbano, Nicolas Padilla, and Stephan Meier, "Gender Differences in Preferences for Meaning at Work," Columbia Business School, working paper, March 4, 2020, http://www.columbia.edu/~np2506/papers/burbano_gender_job _preferences_Mar2020.pdf.

12. Tasha Eurich, "What Self-Awareness Really Is (and How to Cultivate It)," *Harvard Business Review*, January 4, 2018, https://hbr.org/2018/01/what-self-awareness -really-is-and-how-to-cultivate-it.

13. Burbano, Padilla, and Meier, "Gender Differences in Preferences for Meaning at Work."

14. Derald Wing Sue, "Microaggression: More Than Just Race," n.d., https://www .uua.org/sites/live-new.uua.org/files/microaggressions_by_derald_wing_sue_ph.d ._.pdf.

15. Kathleen K. Reardon, "Courage as a Skill," *Harvard Business Review*, January 2007, https://hbr.org/2007/01/courage-as-a-skill.

16. Janet Ledesma, "Conceptual Frameworks and Research Models on Resilience in Leadership," *SAGE Open*, August 12, 2014, https://doi.org/10.1177/21582440 14545464.

17. Zhen Wang, Chaoping Li, and Xupei Li, "Resilience, Leadership, and Work Engagement: The Mediating Role of Positive Affect," *Social Indicators Research* 132 (2017): 699–708, https://doi.org/10.1007/s11205-016-1306-5.

18. Signe M. Spencer, E. Susanne Blazek, and J. Evelyn Orr, "Bolstering the Female CEO Pipeline: Equalizing the Playing Field and Igniting Women's Potential as Top-Level Leaders," *Business Horizons* 62, no. 5 (2019): 567–577.

19. Laura Morgan Roberts, Anthony J. Mayo, Robin J. Ely, and David A. Thomas, "Beating the Odds: Leadership Lessons from Senior African-American Women," *Harvard Business Review*, March–April 2018, https://hbr.org/2018/03/beating-the -odds.

20. Ibarra, Ely, and Kolb, "Women Rising."

Chapter 3

1. Two recent studies have found that women are younger than their male counterparts when appointed CEO. One study in 2017 found that women CEOs are around two years younger than their male counterparts (see Pradit Withisuphakorn and Pornsit Jiraporn, "CEO Age and CEO Gender: Are Female CEOs Older Than Their Male Counterparts?," *Finance Research Letters* 22 [2017]: 129–135). A survey by LinkedIn in 2019 found similar findings, albeit with a slightly smaller gap of just 1.4 years (Kristin Keveloh and Rachel Bowley, "Faster but Fewer: The [Small] Window in the Glass Ceiling," LinkedIn Economic Graph, March 8, 2019, https://economic graph.linkedin.com/blog/faster-but-fewer-the-small-window-in-the-glass-ceiling1).

2. Vanessa Fuhrmans, "Where Women Fall Behind at Work: The First Step into Management," *Wall Street Journal*, October 15, 2019, https://www.wsj.com/articles /where-women-fall-behind-at-work-the-first-step-into-management-11571112361.

3. See Ted H. Shore, "Subtle Gender Bias in the Assessment of Managerial Potential," *Sex Roles* 27 (1992): 499–515, as well as Robin J. Ely, Herminia Ibarra, and Deborah M. Kolb, "Taking Gender into Account: Theory and Design for Women's Leadership Development Programs," *Academy of Management Learning & Education* 10 (2012): 474–493, https://doi.org/10.5465/amle.2010.0046.

4. Abigail Player, Georgina Randsley de Moura, Ana C. Leite, Dominic Abrams, and Fatima Tresh, "Overlooked Leadership Potential: The Preference for Leadership

Potential in Job Candidates Who Are Men vs. Women," *Frontiers in Psychology* 10 (2019): article 755, https://doi.org/10.3389/fpsyg.2019.00755.

5. Player et al., "Overlooked Leadership Potential."

6. Carol Geffner and Joy White, "My Leadership Journey: Joy White, Executive Director, Space and Missile Systems Center," *Executive Master Leadership Blog*, University of Southern California, July 24, 2018, https://eml.usc.edu/blog/leadership-journey-interview-with-joy-white.

7. Michelle K. Ryan and S. Alexander Haslam, "The Glass Cliff: Exploring the Dynamics Surrounding the Appointment of Women to Precarious Leadership Positions," *Academy of Management Review* 32, no. 2 (2007): 549–572, http://www.jstor.org/stable/20159315.

8. McKinsey & Company / Lean In, *Women in the Workplace 2020* (N.p.: McKinsey & Company, 2020), https://wiw-report.s3.amazonaws.com/Women_in_the_Workplace_2020.pdf.

9. An article published in the *New York Times* in May 2020, for example, pitted New Zealand's Jacinda Ardern's approach to the pandemic against President Donald Trump's approach. As the article observed, while President Trump was anthropomorphizing the virus as a foe and rejecting guidance from the Centers for Disease Control and Prevention, Ms. Ardern was addressing her nation in Facebook Live sessions from her family home and expressing empathy with citizens' anxieties as they adjusted to lockdown (see Amanda Taub, "Why Are Nations Led by Women Doing Better?," *New York Times*, May 16, 2020).

10. Ryan and Haslam, "The Glass Cliff," 553.

11. Ryan and Haslam, "The Glass Cliff," 553.

12. Ken Shepherd, "Marissa Mayer Leaves Yahoo with $260M in Severance Pay and Stock: Report," *Washington Times*, June 13, 2017, https://www.washingtontimes.com/news/2017/jun/13/marissa-mayer-leaves-yahoo-260m-severance-pay-and-/.

13. Susan R. Fisk and Jon Overton, "Bold or Reckless? The Impact of Workplace Risk-Taking on Attributions and Expected Outcomes," *PLOS One* 15, no. 3 (March 4, 2020), https://doi.org/10.1371/journal.pone.0228672.

14. See, for example, Jane Edison Stevenson and Evelyn Orr, "We Interviewed 57 Female CEOs to Find Out How More Women Can Get to the Top," *Harvard Business Review*, November 8, 2017, https://hbr.org/2017/11/we-interviewed-57-female-ceos-to-find-out-how-more-women-can-get-to-the-top; Rebecca Ray and Beatrice Gretch-Cumbo, "Tactics to Advance Women in the Leadership Pipeline," Conference Board, 2021, https://www.conference-Board.org/blog/human-capital/Women-Leadership-Advancement-Tactics; and World Economic Forum, "Three Leaders on

Creating a Pipeline for Female Talent in Business," March 2020, https://www.wefo rum.org/agenda/2020/03/3-women-business-leaders-gender-parity-workplace.

15. Paola Cecchi-Dimeglio, "How Gender Bias Corrupts Performance Reviews, and What to Do about It," *Harvard Business Review*, April 12, 2017, https://hbr.org /2017/04/how-gender-bias-corrupts-performance-reviews-and-what-to-do -about-it.

16. See, among other current talent-management platforms, Plum.io. As stated on the company's website, "Most emerging leader assessments are reserved for a select few, but Plum empowers you to invest in the people within every level of your organization. Plum evaluates everyone—from entry-level employees to senior managers—for leadership potential, finding people who may have otherwise floated under your radar and not been considered for a leadership position" (https://www .plum.io/emerging-leaders).

17. Kimberly A. Houser, "Can AI Solve the Diversity Problem in the Tech Industry? Mitigating Noise and Bias in Employment Decision-Making," *Stanford Technology Law Review* 22 (Spring 2019): 290–353, https://www-cdn.law.stanford.edu/wp-con tent/uploads/2019/08/Houser_20190808.pdf.

18. Claudio Fernández-Aráoz, Boris Groysberg, and Nitin Nohria, "How to Hang On to Your High Potentials," *Harvard Business Review*, October 2011, https://hbr.org /2011/10/how-to-hang-on-to-your-high-potentials.

19. See, among other studies, Linda J. Searby, Julia Ballenger, and Jenny Tripses, "Climbing the Ladder, Holding the Ladder: The Mentoring Experiences of Higher Education Female Leaders," *Advancing Women in Leadership* 35 (2015): 98–107; Margaret Linehan and Hugh Scullion, "The Development of Female Global Managers: The Role of Mentoring and Networking," *Journal of Business Ethics* 83 (2008): 29–40, https://doi.org/10.1007/s10551-007-9657-0; and Mary Hale Tolar, "Mentoring Experiences of High-Achieving Women," *Advances in Developing Human Resources* 14, no. 2 (2012): 172–187, https://doi.org/10.1177/1523422312436415.

20. Fernández-Aráoz, Groysberg, and Nohria, "How to Hang On to Your High Potentials."

21. Nancy M. Carter and Christine Silva, *Mentoring: Necessary but Insufficient for Advancement* (New York: Catalyst, 2010). The Catalyst study found that more men than women had a mentor at the CEO or senior executive level (62 percent of men versus 52 percent of women). This difference likely reflects that high-potential men were more likely to choose male mentors (91 percent chose a male versus a female mentor) and that men are more likely to be in CEO positions than women. The same study found that high-potential women were also more likely to choose male mentors, with more than half (65 percent) opting for a male rather than female mentor (3).

22. Kim Parker, "Despite Progress, Women Still Bear a Heavier Load Than Men in Balancing Work and Family," Pew Research Center, March 10, 2015, https://www.pewresearch.org/fact-tank/2015/03/10/women-still-bear-heavier-load-than-men-balancing-work-family/.

23. The authors of McKinsey & Company's *Women in the Workplace 2020* report observe, "Not surprisingly, senior-level women are significantly more likely than men at the same level to feel under pressure to work more and as though they have to be 'always on.' And they are 1.5 times more likely than senior-level men to think about downshifting their careers or leaving the workforce because of Covid-19. Almost 3 in 4 cite burnout as a main reason" (McKinsey & Company / Lean In, *Women in the Workplace 2020* [N.p.: McKinsey & Company, 2020], https://wiw-report.s3.amazonaws.com/Women_in_the_Workplace_2020.pdf).

24. McKinsey & Company / Lean In, *Women in the Workplace 2020*.

25. A study by Kristen Shockley and others in 2017 found that men are nearly as likely as women to suffer from work–family conflicts but also noted that this finding may reflect the fact that more men are now in dual-earner households. See Kristin M. Shockley, Winny Shen, Michael M. DeNunzio, Maryana L. Arvan, and Eric A. Knudsen, "Disentangling the Relationship between Gender and Work–Family Conflict: An Integration of Theoretical Perspectives Using Meta-analytic Methods," *Journal of Applied Psychology* 102, no. 12 (2017): 1601–1635, https://doi.org/10.1037/apl0000246.

26. Prithwiraj (Raj) Choudhury, "Make the Most of Your Relocation," *Harvard Business Review*, July–August 2020, https://hbr.org/2020/07/make-the-most-of-your-relocation.

27. As Mark C. Bolino, Anthony C. Klotz, and William H. Turnley observed in 2017, "Many companies expect their aspiring leaders to work abroad. It's how their executives develop the skills to lead across cultures and learn the inner workings of a global business; it's how rising leaders advance into the senior ranks." However, as they further note, "Those who decline may be perceived to lack ambition and drive, and they may pay a price for that" ("Will Refusing an International Assignment Derail Your Career?," *Harvard Business Review*, April 18, 2017, https://hbr.org/2017/04/will-refusing-an-international-assignment-derail-your-career).

28. McKinsey & Company / Lean In, *Women in the Workplace 2020*.

29. Audre Lorde, "The Master's Tools Will Never Dismantle the Master's House," in *Sister Outsider: Essays and Speeches by Audre Lorde* (New York: Penguin, 1984), 110–113.

30. Douglas Riddle, "Your High-Potential Program Could Ruin Your Business," *Harvard Business Review*, July 17, 2012, https://hbr.org/2012/07/your-high-potential-program.

31. IBM Institute for Business Value, "What Employees Expect in 2021," 2021, https://www.ibm.com/thought-leadership/institute-business-value/report/employee-expectations-2021.

32. Prudential, *Pulse of the American Worker Survey: Is This Working?* (2020), https://news.prudential.com/presskits/pulse-american-worker-survey-is-this-working.htm.

33. Gallup, "How Millennials Want to Work and Live," 2016, https://enviablework place.com/wp-content/uploads/Gallup-How-Millennials-Want-To-Work.pdf.

Chapter 4

1. See, for example, Sidney Jourard, "A Study of Self-Disclosure," *Scientific American* 198 (1958): 77–82; Sidney Jourard and Paul Lasakow, "Some Factors in Self-Disclosure," *Journal of Abnormal and Social Psychology* 56 (1958): 91–98.

2. Irwin A. Berg and Bernard M. Bass, eds., *Conformity and Deviation* (New York: Harper and Row, 1961).

3. Richard M. Drag and Marvin E. Shaw, "Factors Influencing the Communication of Emotional Intent by Facial Expressions," *Psychonomic Science* 8, nos. 137–138 (1967), https://doi.org/10.3758/BF0333158.

4. John E. Baird Jr. and Patricia Hayes Bradley, "Styles of Management and Communication: A Comparative Study of Men and Women," *Communication Monographs* 46, no. 2 (1976): 101.

5. Deborah Tannen, *Talking 9 to 5* (New York: Harper Collins, 1994), 40.

6. Ellen Pao v. Kleiner Perkins Caufield & Byers LLC and DOES 1–20, Supreme Court of the State of California, case no. S212557, filed June 26, 2013.

7. Quoted in Jessica Bennet, "Ellen Pao Is Not Done Fighting," *New York Times*, September 8, 2017, https://www.nytimes.com/2017/09/08/style/ellen-pao-gender-discrimination-silicon-valley-reset.html.

8. Elizabeth J. McClean, Sean R. Martin, Kyle J. Emich, and Todd Woodruff, "The Social Consequences of Voice: An Examination of Voice Type and Gender on Status and Subsequent Leader Emergence," *Academy of Management Journal* 61, no. 5 (2018): 1869–1891, https://doi.org/10.5465/amj.2016.0148.

9. McClean et al., "The Social Consequences of Voice," 1884.

10. J. M. Montepare, "The Impact of Variations in Height on Young Children's Impressions of Men and Women," *Journal of Nonverbal Behavior* 19 (1995): 31–47, https://doi.org/10.1007/BF02173411.

11. Abigail A. Marsh, Henry H. Yu, Julia C. Schechter, and R. J. R. Blair, "Larger Than Life: Humans' Nonverbal Status Cues Alter Perceived Size," *PLOS One* 4, no. 5 (May 27, 2009), https://doi.org/10.1371/journal.pone.0005707.

12. Charles I. Brooks, Michael A. Church, and Lance Fraser, "Effects of Duration of Eye Contact on Judgments of Personality Characteristics," *Journal of Social Psychology* 126, no. 1 (1986): 71–78, https://doi.org/10.1080/00224545.1986.9713572.

13. See, among other research studies, Thomas Grunwald, Manila Vannucci, Nico Pezer, Martin Kurthen, Johannes Schramm, and Christian E. Elger, "Gender Specific Processing of Eye Contact within the Human Medial Temporal Lobe," *Clinical EEG and Neuroscience* 38, no. 3 (2007): 143–147, https://doi.org/10.1177/155005940 703800310.

14. Carol Kinsey Gorman, *The Silent Language of Leaders* (New York: Wiley, 2011), 160–161.

15. Gorman, *The Silent Language of Leaders*, 155–156.

16. Gorman, *The Silent Language of Leaders*, 158–159.

17. Ellen Berten, "Dress to Impress," *Wall Street Journal*, December 14, 2010, https://www.wsj.com/articles/SB10001424052748704694004576019783931381042.

18. Nathan A. Heflick, Jamie L. Goldenberg, Douglas P. Cooper, and Elisa Puvia, "From Women to Objects: Appearance Focus, Target Gender, and Perceptions of Warmth, Morality, and Competence," *Journal of Experimental Social Psychology* 47, no. 3 (2011): 572–581, https://doi.org/10.1016/j.jesp.2010.12.020.

19. See, for example, Kristina Mitchell and Jonathan Martin, "Gender Bias in Student Evaluations," *PS: Political Science & Politics* 51, no. 3 (2018): 648–652, https://doi.org/10.1017/S104909651800001X.

20. Katharine K. Zarrella, "The Most Powerful Women in Business Wear Power Dresses, Not Suits," *Wall Street Journal*, August 29, 2019, https://www.wsj.com/articles/the-most-powerful-women-in-business-wear-dresses-not-suits-11567106879.

21. Tony Schwartz, "What Women Know about Leadership That Men Don't," *Harvard Business Review*, October 30, 2012, https://hbr.org/2012/10/what-women -know-that-men-dont.

22. Bill George, Peter Sims, Andrew N. McLean, and Diana Mayer, "Discovering Your Authentic Leadership," *Harvard Business Review*, February 2007, https://hbr .org/2007/02/discovering-your-authentic-leadership.

23. Helena Liu, Leanne Cutcher, and David Grant, "Doing Authenticity: The Gendered Construction of Authentic Leadership," *Gender, Work, and Organisation* 22, no. 3 (2015): 249, https://doi.org/10.1111/gwao.12073.

24. Liu, Cutcher, and Grant, "Doing Authenticity," 250.

25. Uri Friedman, "New Zealand's Prime Minister May Be the Most Effective Leader on the Planet," *Atlantic*, April 19, 2020, https://www.theatlantic.com/politics/ar chive/2020/04/jacinda-ardern-new-zealand-leadership-coronavirus/610237/.

26. Bill George, "These Coronavirus Heroes Show Us How Crisis Leadership Works," *Working Knowledge*, March 24, 2020, https://hbswk.hbs.edu/item/these-co ronavirus-heroes-show-us-how-crisis-leadership-works.

27. Tina R. Opie and Katherine W. Phillips, "Hair Penalties: The Negative Influence of Afrocentric Hair on Ratings of Black Women's Dominance and Professionalism," *Frontiers in Psychology* 6 (2015), https://doi.org/10.3389/fpsyg.2015.01311.

28. Daniel Goleman and Richard E. Boyatzis, "Emotional Intelligence Has 12 Elements. Which Do You Need to Work On?," *Harvard Business Review*, February 6, 2017, https://hbr.org/2017/02/emotional-intelligence-has-12-elements-which-do-you -need-to-work-on.

29. Tasha Eurich, "Why Self-Awareness Isn't Doing More to Help Women's Careers," *Harvard Business Review*, May 31, 2019, https://hbr.org/2019/05/why-self -awareness-isnt-doing-more-to-help-womens-careers.

30. Eurich, "Why Self-Awareness Isn't Doing More to Help Women's Careers."

31. Ellen Barry, "A College President Worried about the Risks of Dorm Isolation. So He Moved In," *New York Times*, March 4, 2021, https://www.nytimes.com/2021 /03/04/us/norwich-university-president-dormitory.html.

32. Jim Collins, *Good to Great* (New York: Harper Collins, 2001).

33. Bradley P. Owens and David R. Hekman, "Modeling How to Grow: An Inductive Examination of Humble Leader Behaviors, Contingencies, and Outcomes," *Academy of Management Journal* 55, no. 4 (August 2012): 797.

34. Zuhairah Washington and Laura Morgan Roberts, "Women of Color Get Less Support at Work. Here's How Managers Can Change That," *Harvard Business Review*, March 4, 2019, https://hbr.org/2019/03/women-of-color-get-less-support-at-work -heres-how-managers-can-change-that.

35. Victoria L. Brescoll, "Who Takes the Floor and Why: Gender, Power, and Volubility in Organizations," *Administrative Science Quarterly* 56, no. 4 (2011): 622–641.

36. Leslie Pratch and Jordan Jacobowitz, "Gender, Motivation, and Coping in the Evaluation of Leadership Effectiveness," *Consulting Psychology Journal: Practice and Research* 48, no. 4 (1996): 217, https://doi.org/10.1037/1061-4087.48.4.203.

37. Emily Peck, "Women at Ernst & Young Instructed on How to Dress, Act Nicely around Men," *HuffPost*, October 21, 2019, https://www.huffpost.com/entry/women -ernst-young-how-to-dress-act-around-men_n_5da721eee4b002e33e78606a.

38. Peck, "Women at Ernst & Young Instructed on How to Dress."

39. Frank Dobbin, Alexandra Kalev, and Erin Kelly, "Diversity Management in Corporate America," *Contexts* 6, no. 4 (2007): 21–27.

40. Frank Dobbin and Alexandra Kalev, "Why Doesn't Diversity Training Work?," *Anthropology Now*, May 4, 2018, 48–55.

41. Laura Liswood, "Women Directors Change How Boards Work," *Harvard Business Review*, February 17, 2015, https://hbr.org/2015/02/women-directors-change-how -Boards-work.

42. Kim Parker, Nikki Graf, and Ruth Igielnik, "Generation Z Looks a Lot Like Millennials on Key Social and Political Issues," Pew Research Center, January 17, 2019, https://www.pewresearch.org/social-trends/2019/01/17/generation-z-looks-a-lot -like-millennials-on-key-social-and-political-issues/.

43. Deloitte, "Welcome to Generation Z," 2019, https://www2.deloitte.com/con tent/dam/Deloitte/us/Documents/consumer-business/welcome-to-gen-z.pdf.

44. Emma Goldberg, "The 37-Year-Olds Are Afraid of the 23-Year-Olds Who Work for Them," *New York Times*, October 28, 2021, https://www.nytimes.com/2021/10 /28/business/gen-z-workplace-culture.html.

Chapter 5

1. Inga Carboni and Rob Cross, "The Secrets of Successful Female Networkers," *Harvard Business Review*, November–December 2019, https://hbr.org/2019/11/the -secrets-of-successful-female-networkers.

2. Lisa C. Ehrich, "Mentoring and Women Managers: Another Look at the Field," *Gender in Management* 23, no. 7 (2008): 479.

3. David Clutterbuck, *Everyone Needs a Mentor: Fostering Talent in Your Organisation*, 4th ed. (London: Chartered Institute of Personnel and Development, 2004).

4. Ehrich, "Mentoring and Women Managers," 470.

5. Ehrich, "Mentoring and Women Managers," 470.

6. Linehan and Scullion, "The Development of Female Global Managers," 37.

7. Marilyn M. Helms, Deborah Elwell Arfken, and Stephanie Bellar, "The Importance of Mentoring and Sponsorship in Women's Career Development," *SAM Advanced Management Journal* 81, no. 3 (2016): 17.

8. Helms, Arfken, and Bellar, "The Importance of Mentoring and Sponsorship in Women's Career Development," 17.

9. Jane Greene and Anthony M. Grant, *Solution-Focused Coaching: Managing People in a Complex World* (London: Chartered Institute of Personnel and Development, 2006), 1.

10. International Coaching Federation (ICF), "ICF Global Coaching Client Study," 2009, https://researchportal.coachfederation.org/Document/Pdf/abstract_190.

11. Ronald J. Burke and Deborah L. Nelson, *Advancing Women's Careers* (Malden, MA: Blackwell, 2002), 213.

12. Deborah O'Neil, Margaret M. Hopkins, and Diane Bilimoria, "A Framework for Developing Women Leaders: Applications to Executive Coaching," *Journal of Applied Behavioral Science* 51, no. 2 (2015): 253–276.

13. O'Neil, Hopkins, and Bilimoria, "A Framework for Developing Women Leaders," 271.

14. Ahu Yildirmaz, Christopher Ryan, and Jeff Nezaj, *2019 State of the Workforce Report* (Roseland, NJ: ADP Research Institute, 2019), https://www.adpri.org/assets/2019-state-of-the-workforce-report/.

15. Quoted in Adam Liptak, "J. P. Frank, 84, a Lawyer in Landmark Cases, Dies," *New York Times*, September 10, 2002, https://www.nytimes.com/2002/09/10/us/j-p-frank-84-a-lawyer-in-landmark-cases-dies.html.

16. Collette Stallbaumer and Marissa King, "Work Friends: What the Research Says about Our Ties with Colleagues," *Perspectives* (Microsoft Worklab), n.d., https://www.microsoft.com/en-us/worklab/work-friends.

17. Quoted in Hailey Fuchs, "Doug Emhoff Embraces His Role as the First Second Gentleman," *New York Times*, January 21, 2021.

18. Avivah Wittenberg-Cox, "If You Can't Find a Spouse Who Supports Your Career, Stay Single," *Harvard Business Review*, October 24, 2017, https://hbr.org/2017/10/if-you-cant-find-a-spouse-who-supports-your-career-stay-single.

19. Pamela Stone and Meg Lovejoy, "Fast-Track Women and the 'Choice' to Stay Home," *Annals of the American Academy of Political and Social Science* 596, no. 1 (2004): 62–83, doi:10.1177/0002716204268552.

20. McKinsey & Company, "Seven Charts That Show Covid-19's Impact on Women's Employment," March 8, 2021, https://www.mckinsey.com/featured-insights/diversity-and-inclusion/seven-charts-that-show-covid-19s-impact-on-womens-employment#.

21. Wittenberg-Cox, "If You Can't Find a Spouse Who Supports Your Career, Stay Single."

22. Olle Folke and Johanna Rickne, "All the Single Ladies: Job Promotions and the Durability of Marriage," *American Economic Journal: Applied Economics* 12, no. 1 (2020): 260–287.

23. James B. Stewart, "A CEO's Support System, aka Husband," *New York Times*, November 4, 2011, https://www.nytimes.com/2011/11/05/business/a-ceos-support-system-a-k-a-husband.html.

24. Andrew O'Connell, "The One Thing about Your Spouse's Personality That Really Affects Your Career," *Harvard Business Review*, March 2015, https://hbr.org/2014/11/the-one-thing-about-your-spouses-personality-that-affects-your-career.

25. Robert D. Mare, "Educational Homogamy in Two Gilded Ages: Evidence from Inter-generational Social Mobility Data," *Annals of the American Academy of Political and Social Science* 663, no. 1 (2016): 117–139, https://doi.org/10.1177/000271 6215596967.

26. Carboni and Cross, "The Secrets of Successful Female Networkers."

27. Andromachi Athanasopoulou, Amanda Moss Cowan, Michael Smets, and Timothy Morris, "In Interviews, Female CEOs Say They Don't Expect Much Support—at Home or at Work," *Harvard Business Review*, June 15, 2018, https://hbr.org/2018/06/in-interviews-female-ceos-say-they-dont-expect-much-support-at-home-or-at-work.

28. Laura Vanderkam, *I know How She Does It: How Successful Women Make the Most of Their Time* (New York: Portfolio, 2017), 19.

29. Jack Zenger and Joseph Folkman, "Research: Women Score Higher Than Men in Most Leadership Skills," *Harvard Business Review*, June 25, 2018, https://hbr.org/2019/06/research-women-score-higher-than-men-in-most-leadership-skills?registration=success.

30. Rose Marcario, "Why Should Employers Care About Families?," Patagonia, n.d., https://www.patagonia.com/stories/why-should-employers-care-about-families/story-30845.html.

Chapter 6

1. Catalyst, "How Women CEOs Are Selected and Succession," April 2, 2020, https://www.catalyst.org/research/women-ceos-selection-succession/.

2. Anna Nicolaou, James Fontanella-Khan, and Arash Massoudi, "Avon Chief Sheri McCoy to Step Down," *Financial Times*, June 15, 2017, https://www.ft.com/content/55a3c52e-51f6-11e7-bfb8-997009366969.

3. Tripp Mickle, "Reynolds American CEO to Leave Role at Year's End," *Wall Street Journal*, October 19, 2016, https://www.wsj.com/articles/reynolds-american-ceo-to-leave-role-at-years-end-1476880151.

4. Rick Seltzer, "The Slowly Diversifying Presidency," *Inside Higher Education*, June 20, 2017, https://www.insidehighered.com/news/2017/06/20/college-presidents-diversifying-slowly-and-growing-older-study-finds.

5. Cristina González, "Leadership, Succession Planning, and Diversity in Academia," Center for Studies in Higher Education Research & Occasional Paper Series no. 8.10, May 2010, https://escholarship.org/content/qt594483fq/qt594483fq.pdf.

6. Claudio Fernández-Aráoz, Gregory Nagel, and Carrie Green, "The High Cost of Poor Succession Planning," *Harvard Business Review*, May–June 2021, https://hbr.org/2021/05/the-high-cost-of-poor-succession-planning.

7. Fernández-Aráoz, Nagel, and Green, "The High Cost of Poor Succession Planning."

8. Victoria Luby and Jane Edison Stevenson, "7 Tenets of a Good CEO Succession Process," *Harvard Business Review*, December 7, 2016, https://hbr.org/2016/12/7-tenets-of-a-good-ceo-succession-process.

9. Stephanie Bradley Smith, "How a Lack of Sponsorship Keeps Black Women Out of the C-Suite," *Harvard Business Review*, March 5, 2021, https://hbr.org/2021/03/how-a-lack-of-sponsorship-keeps-black-women-out-of-the-c-suite.

10. Anne Mulcahy, "How I Did It: Xerox's Former CEO on Why Succession Shouldn't Be a Horse Race," *Harvard Business Review*, October 2010, https://hbr.org/2010/10/how-i-did-it-xeroxs-former-ceo-on-why-succession-shouldnt-be-a-horse-race.

11. Mulcahy, "How I Did It."

12. Ursula Burns, *Where You Are Is Not Who You Are* (New York: Harper Collins, 2021).

13. Mulcahy, "How I Did It."

14. Mulcahy, "How I Did It."

Conclusion

1. McKinsey & Company / Lean In, *Women in the Workplace 2020* (N.p.: McKinsey & Company, 2020), https://wiw-report.s3.amazonaws.com/Women_in_the_Workplace_2020.pdf.

2. IBM, "Women, Leadership, and Missed Opportunities," 2021, https://www.ibm.com/thought-leadership/institute-business-value/report/women-leadership-2021.

3. National Women's Law Center, "Another 275,000 Women Left the Labor Force in January," February 5, 2021, https://nwlc.org/resources/january-jobs-day -2021/.

4. Dawn Desjardins and Carrie Freestone, "COVID Further Clouded the Outlook for Canadian Women at Risk of Disruption," *RBC Human Capital*, March 4, 2021, https://thoughtleadership.rbc.com/covid-further-clouded-the-outlook-for-canadian -women-at-risk-of-disruption/?utm_medium=referral&utm_source=media&utm _campaign=special+report.

Bibliography

American Council on Education. *American College President Study*. Washington, DC: American Council on Education, 2017. https://www.aceacps.org/women-presidents /#demographics.

Amoruso, Sophia. *#Girlboss*. New York: Penguin, 2014.

Athanasopoulou, Andromachi, Amanda Moss Cowan, Michael Smets, and Timothy Morris. "In Interviews, Female CEOs Say They Don't Expect Much Support—at Home or at Work." *Harvard Business Review*, June 15, 2018. https://hbr.org/2018/06 /in-interviews-female-ceos-say-they-dont-expect-much-support-at-home-or-at-work.

Baird, John E., Jr., and Patricia Hayes Bradley. "Styles of Management and Communication: A Comparative Study of Men and Women." *Communication Monographs* 46, no. 2 (1976): 101–111.

Barry, Ellen. "A College President Worried about the Risks of Dorm Isolation. So He Moved In." *New York Times*, March 4, 2021. https://www.nytimes.com/2021/03/04 /us/norwich-university-president-dormitory.html.

Bennet, Jessica. "Ellen Pao Is Not Done Fighting." *New York Times*, September 8, 2017. https://www.nytimes.com/2017/09/08/style/ellen-pao-gender-discrimination -silicon-valley-reset.html.

Bensahel, Nora, David Barno, Katherine Kidder, and Kelley Sayler. *Battlefields and Boardrooms: Women's Leadership in the Military and the Private Sector*. Washington, DC: Center for a New American Security, January 2015. https://www.files.ethz.ch /isn/187251/CNAS_BattlefieldsVsBoardrooms_BensahelBarnoKidderSayler.pdf.

Berg, Irwin A., and Bernard M. Bass, eds. *Conformity and Deviation*. New York: Harper and Row, 1961.

Berten, Ellen. "Dress to Impress." *Wall Street Journal*, December 14, 2010. https://www.wsj.com/articles/SB10001424052748704694004576019783931381042.

Bickett, David, Jochen Schweitzer, and Emmanuel Mastio. "Curiosity in Leadership: A Strategic Paradox." Paper presented at the European Group for Organizational Studies Conference, 2019. https://opus.lib.uts.edu.au/handle/10453/133969.

Bolino, Mark C., Anthony C. Klotz, and William H. Turnley. "Will Refusing an International Assignment Derail Your Career?" *Harvard Business Review*, April 18, 2017. https://hbr.org/2017/04/will-refusing-an-international-assignment-derail-your-career.

Bothwell, Ellie. "Female Leadership in Top Universities Advances for First Time since 2017." *Times Higher Education Supplement*, March 6, 2020. https://www.timeshighereducation.com/news/female-leadership-top-universities-advances-first-time-2017.

Bradley Smith, Stephanie. "How a Lack of Sponsorship Keeps Black Women Out of the C-Suite." *Harvard Business Review*, March 5, 2021. https://hbr.org/2021/03/how-a-lack-of-sponsorship-keeps-black-women-out-of-the-c-suite.

Brescoll, Victoria L. "Who Takes the Floor and Why: Gender, Power, and Volubility in Organizations." *Administrative Science Quarterly* 56, no. 4 (2011): 622–641.

Brooks, Charles I., Michael A. Church, and Lance Fraser. "Effects of Duration of Eye Contact on Judgments of Personality Characteristics." *Journal of Social Psychology* 126, no. 1 (1986): 71–78. https://doi.org/10.1080/00224545.1986.9713572.

Brown, Brené. *Dare to Lead*. New York: Random House, 2018.

Burbano, Vanessa, Nicolas Padilla, and Stephan Meier. "Gender Differences in Preferences for Meaning at Work." Columbia Business School, working paper, March 4, 2020. http://www.columbia.edu/~np2506/papers/burbano_gender_job_preferences_Mar2020.pdf.

Burke, Ronald J., and Deborah L. Nelson. *Advancing Women's Careers*. Malden, MA: Blackwell, 2002.

Burns, Ursula. *Where You Are Is Not Who You Are*. New York: Harper Collins, 2021.

Campuzano, Mariella V. "Force and Inertia: A Systematic Review of Women's Leadership in Male-Dominated Organizational Cultures in the United States." *Human Resource Development Review* 18, no. 4 (2019): 437–469. https://doi.org/10.1177/1534484319861169.

Carboni, Inga, and Rob Cross. "The Secrets of Successful Female Networkers." *Harvard Business Review*, November–December 2019. https://hbr.org/2019/11/the-secrets-of-successful-female-networkers.

Carreyrou, John. "Hot Startup Theranos Has Struggled With Its Blood-Test Technology." *Wall Street Journal*, last updated October 16, 2015. https://www.wsj.com/arti cles/theranos-has-struggled-with-blood-tests-1444881901.

Carter, Nancy M., and Christine Silva. *Mentoring: Necessary but Insufficient for Advancement*. New York: Catalyst, 2010.

Catalyst. "Historical List of Women CEOs of the Fortune Lists: 1972–2020." June 2019. https://www.catalyst.org/wp-content/uploads/2019/06/Catalyst_Women_Fortune _CEOs_1972-2020_Historical_List_5.28.2020.pdf.

Catalyst. "How Women CEOs Are Selected and Succession." April 2, 2020. https:// www.catalyst.org/research/women-ceos-selection-succession/.

Cecchi-Dimeglio, Paola. "How Gender Bias Corrupts Performance Reviews, and What to Do about It." *Harvard Business Review*, April 12, 2017. https://hbr.org/2017/04 /how-gender-bias-corrupts-performance-reviews-and-what-to-do-about-it.

Choudhury, Prithwiraj (Raj). "Make the Most of Your Relocation." *Harvard Business Review*, July–August 2020. https://hbr.org/2020/07/make-the-most-of-your-relocation.

Clark, Kate. "US VC Investment in Female Founders Hits All-Time High." *Tech-Crunch*, December 9, 2019. https://techcrunch.com/2019/12/09/us-vc-investment -in-female-founders-hits-all-time-high/.

Clutterbuck, David. *Everyone Needs a Mentor: Fostering Talent in Your Organisation*. 4th ed. London: Chartered Institute of Personnel and Development, 2004.

Collins, Jim. *Good to Great*. New York: Harper Collins, 2001.

Council for Foreign Relations. "Demographics of the U.S. Military." July 13, 2020. https://www.cfr.org/backgrounder/demographics-us-military.

Deloitte. "Welcome to Generation Z." 2019. https://www2.deloitte.com/content /dam/Deloitte/us/Documents/consumer-business/welcome-to-gen-z.pdf.

Deloitte. *Women in the Board Room: A Global Perspective*. 6th ed. London: Deloitte, 2019. https://www2.deloitte.com/content/dam/Deloitte/global/Documents/Risk/gx -risk-women-in-the-Boardroom-sixth-edition.pdf.

Desjardins, Dawn, and Carrie Freestone. "COVID Further Clouded the Outlook for Canadian Women at Risk of Disruption." *RBC Human Capital*, March 4, 2021. https://thoughtleadership.rbc.com/covid-further-clouded-the-outlook-for-canadian -women-at-risk-of-disruption/?utm_medium=referral&utm_source=media&utm _campaign=special+report.

Dobbin, Frank, and Alexandra Kalev. "Why Doesn't Diversity Training Work?" *Anthropology Now*, May 4, 2018, 48–55.

Dobbin, Frank, Alexandra Kalev, and Erin Kelly. "Diversity Management in Corporate America." *Contexts* 6, no. 4 (2007): 21–27.

Drag, Richard M., and Marvin E. Shaw. "Factors Influencing the Communication of Emotional Intent by Facial Expressions." *Psychonomic Science* 8 (1967): 137–138. https://doi.org/10.3758/BF0333158.

Ehrich, Lisa C. "Mentoring and Women Managers: Another Look at the Field." *Gender in Management* 23, no. 7 (2008): 469–483.

Ely, Robin J., Herminia Ibarra, and Deborah M. Kolb. "Taking Gender into Account: Theory and Design for Women's Leadership Development Programs." *Academy of Management Learning & Education* 10 (2012): 474–493. https://doi.org/10.5465/amle.2010.0046.

Eurich, Tasha. "What Self-Awareness Really Is (and How to Cultivate It)." *Harvard Business Review*, January 4, 2018. https://hbr.org/2018/01/what-self-awareness-really-is-and-how-to-cultivate-it.

Eurich, Tasha. "Why Self-Awareness Isn't Doing More to Help Women's Careers." *Harvard Business Review*, May 31, 2019. https://hbr.org/2019/05/why-self-awareness-isnt-doing-more-to-help-womens-careers.

Fernández-Aráoz, Claudio, Boris Groysberg, and Nitin Nohria. "How to Hang On to Your High Potentials." *Harvard Business Review*, October 2011. https://hbr.org/2011/10/how-to-hang-on-to-your-high-potentials.

Fernández-Aráoz, Claudio, Gregory Nagel, and Carrie Green. "The High Cost of Poor Succession Planning." *Harvard Business Review*, May–June 2021. https://hbr.org/2021/05/the-high-cost-of-poor-succession-planning.

Fine, Marlene G. "Women Leaders' Discursive Constructions of Leadership." *Women's Studies in Communication* 32, no. 2 (2009): 180–202.

Fisher, Melissa. "Wall Street Women: Professional Saviors of the Global Economy." *Critical Perspectives on International Business* 11 (2015): 137–155.

Fisk, Susan R., and Jon Overton. "Bold or Reckless? The Impact of Workplace Risk-Taking on Attributions and Expected Outcomes." *PLOS One* 15, no. 3 (March 4, 2020). https://doi.org/10.1371/journal.pone.0228672.

Folke, Olle, and Johanna Rickne. "All the Single Ladies: Job Promotions and the Durability of Marriage." *American Economic Journal: Applied Economics* 12, no. 1 (2020): 260–287.

Fowler, Susan. "Reflecting on One Very, Very Strange Year at Uber." *SusanFowler.com* (blog), February 19, 2017. https://www.susanjfowler.com/blog/2017/2/19/reflecting-on-one-very-strange-year-at-uber.

Friedman, Uri. "New Zealand's Prime Minister May Be the Most Effective Leader on the Planet." *Atlantic*, April 19, 2020. https://www.theatlantic.com/politics/archive /2020/04/jacinda-ardern-new-zealand-leadership-coronavirus/610237/.

Fuchs, Hailey. "Doug Emhoff Embraces His Role as the First Second Gentleman." *New York Times*, January 21, 2021.

Fuhrmans, Vanessa. "Where Women Fall Behind at Work: The First Step into Management." *Wall Street Journal*, October 15, 2019. https://www.wsj.com/articles/where -women-fall-behind-at-work-the-first-step-into-management-11571112361.

Gallup. "How Millennials Want to Work and Live." 2016. https://enviablework place.com/wp-content/uploads/Gallup-How-Millennials-Want-To-Work.pdf.

Geffner, Carol, and Joy White. "My Leadership Journey: Joy White, Executive Director, Space and Missile Systems Center." *Executive Master Leadership Blog*, University of Southern California, July 24, 2018. https://eml.usc.edu/blog/leadership -journey-interview-with-joy-white.

George, Bill. *Authentic Leadership: Rediscovering the Secrets to Creating Lasting Value.* San Francisco: Jossey-Bass, 2003.

George, Bill. *Discover Your True North*. San Francisco: Jossey-Bass, 2007.

George, Bill. "These Coronavirus Heroes Show Us How Crisis Leadership Works." *Working Knowledge*, March 24, 2020. https://hbswk.hbs.edu/item/these-coronavirus -heroes-show-us-how-crisis-leadership-works.

George, Bill, Peter Sims, Andrew N. McLean, and Diana Mayer. "Discovering Your Authentic Leadership." *Harvard Business Review*, February 2007. https://hbr.org/2007 /02/discovering-your-authentic-leadership.

Gino, Francesca. "The Business Case for Curiosity." *Harvard Business Review*, September–October 2018. https://hbr.org/2018/09/the-business-case-for-curiosity.

Goldberg, Emma. "The 37-Year-Olds Are Afraid of the 23-Year-Olds Who Work for Them." *New York Times*, October 28, 2021. https://www.nytimes.com/2021/10/28 /business/gen-z-workplace-culture.html.

Goleman, Daniel, and Richard E. Boyatzis. "Emotional Intelligence Has 12 Elements. Which Do You Need to Work On?" *Harvard Business Review*, February 6, 2017. https://hbr.org/2017/02/emotional-intelligence-has-12-elements-which-do-you -need-to-work-on.

González, Cristina. "Leadership, Succession Planning, and Diversity in Academia." Center for Studies in Higher Education Research & Occasional Paper Series no. 8.10, May 2010. https://escholarship.org/content/qt594483fq/qt594483fq.pdf.

Gorman, Carol Kinsey. *The Silent Language of Leaders*. New York: Wiley, 2011.

Greene, Jane, and Anthony M. Grant. *Solution-Focused Coaching: Managing People in a Complex World*. London: Chartered Institute of Personnel and Development, 2006.

Grunwald, Thomas, Manila Vannucci, Nico Pezer, Martin Kurthen, Johannes Schramm, and Christian E. Elger. "Gender Specific Processing of Eye Contact within the Human Medial Temporal Lobe." *Clinical EEG and Neuroscience* 38, no. 3 (2007): 143–147. https://doi.org/10.1177/155005940703800310.

Harvey, Michael, Milorad Novicevic, Nancy Leonard, and Dinah Payne. "The Role of Curiosity in Global Managers' Decision-Making." *Journal of Leadership & Organizational Studies* 13, no. 3 (2007): 43–58. https://doi.org/10.1177/10717919070130030401.

Hathaway, Ian. "The Ascent of Women-Led Venture-Backed Startups in the United States." Center for American Entrepreneurship, 2017. http://www.startupsusa.org/women-founded-venture-backed-startups/.

Heflick, Nathan A., Jamie L. Goldenberg, Douglas P. Cooper, and Elisa Puvia. "From Women to Objects: Appearance Focus, Target Gender, and Perceptions of Warmth, Morality, and Competence." *Journal of Experimental Social Psychology* 47, no. 3 (2011): 572–581. https://doi.org/10.1016/j.jesp.2010.12.020.

Helms, Marilyn M., Deborah Elwell Arfken, and Stephanie Bellar. "The Importance of Mentoring and Sponsorship in Women's Career Development." *SAM Advanced Management Journal* 81, no. 3 (2016): 4–16.

hooks, bell. "Dig Deep: Beyond Lean In." *Feminist Wire*, October 28, 2013. https://thefeministwire.com/2013/10/17973/.

Houser, Kimberly A. "Can AI Solve the Diversity Problem in the Tech Industry? Mitigating Noise and Bias in Employment Decision-Making." *Stanford Technology Law Review* 22 (Spring 2019): 290–353. https://www-cdn.law.stanford.edu/wp-content/uploads/2019/08/Houser_20190808.pdf.

Hyland, Shelley S., and Elizabeth Davis. *Local Police Departments, 2016: Personnel*. Washington, DC: US Department of Justice, Bureau of Justice Statistics, 2016. https://www.bjs.gov/content/pub/pdf/lpd16p.pdf.

Ibarra, Herminia, Robin Ely, and Deborah Kolb. "Women Rising: The Unseen Barriers." *Harvard Business Review*, September 2013. http://dx.doi.org/10.2469/dig.v43.n5.1.

IBM. "Women, Leadership, and Missed Opportunities." 2021. https://www.ibm.com/thought-leadership/institute-business-value/report/women-leadership-2021.

IBM Institute for Business Value. "What Employees Expect in 2021." 2021. https://www.ibm.com/thought-leadership/institute-business-value/report/employee-expectations-2021.

International Coaching Federation (ICF). "ICF Global Coaching Client Study, Executive Summary." 2009. https://researchportal.coachfederation.org/Document/Pdf/abstract_190.

Jourard, Sidney. "A Study of Self-Disclosure." *Scientific American* 198 (1958): 77–82.

Jourard, Sidney, and Paul Lasakow. "Some Factors in Self-Disclosure." *Journal of Abnormal and Social Psychology* 56 (1958): 91–98.

Keveloh, Kristin, and Rachel Bowley. "Faster but Fewer: The (Small) Window in the Glass Ceiling." LinkedIn Economic Graph, March 8, 2019. https://economicgraph.linkedin.com/blog/faster-but-fewer-the-small-window-in-the-glass-ceiling1.

Kissinger, Henry A. "Elizabeth Holmes." *Time*, April 16, 2015. https://time.com/collection-post/3822734/elizabeth-holmes-2015-time-100/.

Korn Ferry. "No Room at the Top." Survey, May 23, 2019. https://www.kornferry.com/about-us/press/no-room-at-the-top.

KPMG. *Women's Leadership Study*. London: KPMG, 2014. https://assets.kpmg/content/dam/kpmg/ph/pdf/ThoughtLeadershipPublications/KPMGWomensLeadershipStudy.pdf.

Latu, Ioana M., Marianne Schmid Mast, Dario Bombari, Joris Lammers, and Crystal L. Hoyt. "Empowering Mimicry: Female Leader Role Models Empower Women in Leadership Tasks through Body Posture Mimicry." *Sex Roles* 80, no. 1 (2019): 11–24. https://doi.org/10.1007/s11199-018-0911-y.

Ledesma, Janet. "Conceptual Frameworks and Research Models on Resilience in Leadership." *SAGE Open*, August 12, 2014. https://doi.org/10.1177/2158244014545464.

Lev-Ram, Michal. "Theranos' Elizabeth Holmes Calls on Women to Help Each Other." *Fortune*, October 12, 2015. https://fortune.com/2015/10/12/elizabeth-holmes-calls-on-women/.

Linehan, Margaret, and Hugh Scullion. "The Development of Female Global Managers: The Role of Mentoring and Networking." *Journal of Business Ethics* 83 (2008): 29–40. https://doi.org/10.1007/s10551-007-9657-0.

Liptak, Adam. "J. P. Frank, 84, a Lawyer in Landmark Cases, Dies." *New York Times*, September 10, 2002. https://www.nytimes.com/2002/09/10/us/j-p-frank-84-a-lawyer-in-landmark-cases-dies.html.

Liswood, Laura. "Women Directors Change How Boards Work." *Harvard Business Review*, February 17, 2015. https://hbr.org/2015/02/women-directors-change-how-Boards-work.

Liu, Helena, Leanne Cutcher, and David Grant. "Doing Authenticity: The Gendered Construction of Authentic Leadership." *Gender, Work, and Organisation* 22, no. 3 (2015): 237–255. https://doi.org/10.1111/gwao.12073.

Lorde, Audre. "The Master's Tools Will Never Dismantle the Master's House." In *Sister Outsider: Essays and Speeches by Audre Lorde*, 110–113. New York: Penguin, 1984.

Luby, Victoria, and Jane Edison Stevenson. "7 Tenets of a Good CEO Succession Process." *Harvard Business Review*, December 7, 2016. https://hbr.org/2016/12/7 -tenets-of-a-good-ceo-succession-process.

Marcario, Rose. "Why Should Employers Care About Families?" Patagonia, n.d. https://www.patagonia.com/stories/why-should-employers-care-about-families /story-30845.html.

Macaulay, Fiona. "The Surprising Benefits When Men Mentor Women." *Inc.*, April 10, 2019. https://www.inc.com/fiona-macaulay/advice-for-men-who-are-uncertain -about-mentoring-women.html.

Mare, Robert D. "Educational Homogamy in Two Gilded Ages: Evidence from Inter-generational Social Mobility Data." *ANNALS of the American Academy of Political and Social Science* 663, no. 1 (2016): 117–139. https://doi.org/10.1177 /0002716215596967.

Marsh, Abigail A., Henry H. Yu, Julia C. Schechter, and R. J. R. Blair. "Larger Than Life: Humans' Nonverbal Status Cues Alter Perceived Size." *PLOS One* 4, no. 5 (May 27, 2009). https://doi.org/10.1371/journal.pone.0005707.

McClean, Elizabeth J., Sean R. Martin, Kyle J. Emich, and Todd Woodruff. "The Social Consequences of Voice: An Examination of Voice Type and Gender on Status and Subsequent Leader Emergence." *Academy of Management Journal* 61, no. 5 (2018): 1869–1891. https://doi.org/10.5465/amj.2016.0148.

McKinnon, Merryn, and Christine O'Connell. "Perceptions of Stereotypes Applied to Women Who Publicly Communicate Their STEM Work." *Humanities and Social Science Communications* 7 (2020): article 160. https://doi.org/10.1057/s41599-020 -00654-0.

McKinsey & Company. "Seven Charts That Show Covid-19's Impact on Women's Employment." March 8, 2021. https://www.mckinsey.com/featured-insights/diversity -and-inclusion/seven-charts-that-show-covid-19s-impact-on-womens-employment#.

McKinsey & Company / Lean In. *Women in the Workplace 2020*. N.p.: McKinsey & Company, 2020. https://wiw-report.s3.amazonaws.com/Women_in_the_Workplace _2020.pdf.

Mickle, Tripp. "Reynolds American CEO to Leave Role at Year's End." *Wall Street Journal*, October 19, 2016. https://www.wsj.com/articles/reynolds-american-ceo-to -leave-role-at-years-end-1476880151.

Miller, Stephen. "CHRO Pay Trails Other Top Executives." SHRM, October 3, 2016. https://www.shrm.org/resourcesandtools/hr-topics/compensation/pages/chro-pay-trails.aspx.

Mitchell, Kristina, and Jonathan Martin. "Gender Bias in Student Evaluations." *PS: Political Science & Politics* 51, no. 3 (2018): 648–652. https://doi.org/10.1017/S104909651800001X.

Montepare, J. M. "The Impact of Variations in Height on Young Children's Impressions of Men and Women." *Journal of Nonverbal Behavior* 19 (1995): 31–47. https://doi.org/10.1007/BF02173411.

Morgan Roberts, Laura, Anthony J. Mayo, Robin J. Ely, and David A. Thomas. "Beating the Odds: Leadership Lessons from Senior African-American Women." *Harvard Business Review*, March–April 2018. https://hbr.org/2018/03/beating-the-odds.

Muhlhausen, David B. *Women in Policing: Breaking Barriers and Blazing a Path*. Washington, DC: National Institute of Justice, 2019. https://www.ncjrs.gov/pdffiles1/nij/252963.pdf.

Mulcahy, Anne. "How I Did It: Xerox's Former CEO on Why Succession Shouldn't Be a Horse Race." *Harvard Business Review*, October 2010. https://hbr.org/2010/10/how-i-did-it-xeroxs-former-ceo-on-why-succession-shouldnt-be-a-horse-race.

National Women's Law Center. "Another 275,000 Women Left the Labor Force in January." February 5, 2021. https://nwlc.org/resources/january-jobs-day-2021/.

Newman, Judith. "'Lean In': Five Years Later." *New York Times*, March 16, 2018. https://www.nytimes.com/2018/03/16/business/lean-in-five-yearslater.html#:~:text=It%20rode%20the%20New%20York,all%20formats)%2C%20landed%20Ms.

Nicolaou, Anna, James Fontanella-Khan, and Arash Massoudi. "Avon Chief Sheri McCoy to Step Down." *Financial Times*, June 15, 2017. https://www.ft.com/content/55a3c52e-51f6-11e7-bfb8-997009366969.

Obama, Michelle. *Becoming*. New York: Crown, 2018.

O'Connell, Andrew. "The One Thing about Your Spouse's Personality That Really Affects Your Career." *Harvard Business Review*, March 2015. https://hbr.org/2014/11/the-one-thing-about-your-spouses-personality-that-affects-your-career.

O'Neil, Deborah, Margaret M. Hopkins, and Diane Bilimoria. "A Framework for Developing Women Leaders: Applications to Executive Coaching." *Journal of Applied Behavioral Science* 51, no. 2 (2015): 253–276.

Opie, T. R., and K. W. Phillips. "Hair Penalties: The Negative Influence of Afrocentric Hair on Ratings of Black Women's Dominance and Professionalism." *Frontiers in Psychology* 6 (2015). https://doi.org/10.3389/fpsyg.2015.01311.

Owens, Bradley P., and David R. Hekman. "Modeling How to Grow: An Inductive Examination of Humble Leader Behaviors, Contingencies, and Outcomes." *Academy of Management Journal* 55, no. 4 (August 2012): 787–818.

Pace, Cindy. "How Women of Color Get to Senior Management." *Harvard Business Review*, August 31, 2018. https://hbr.org/2018/08/how-women-of-color-get-to -senior-management.

Parker, Kim. "Despite Progress, Women Still Bear a Heavier Load Than Men in Balancing Work and Family." Pew Research Center, March 10, 2015. https://www .pewresearch.org/fact-tank/2015/03/10/women-still-bear-heavier-load-than-men -balancing-work-family/.

Parker, Kim, Nikki Graf, and Ruth Igielnik. "Generation Z Looks a Lot Like Millennials on Key Social and Political Issues." Pew Research Center, January 17, 2019. https://www.pewresearch.org/social-trends/2019/01/17/generation-z-looks-a-lot -like-millennials-on-key-social-and-political-issues/.

Peck, Emily. "Women at Ernst & Young Instructed on How to Dress, Act Nicely around Men." *HuffPost*, October 21, 2019. https://www.huffpost.com/entry/women -ernst-young-how-to-dress-act-around-men_n_5da721eee4b002e33e78606a.

Player, Abigail, Georgina Randsley de Moura, Ana C. Leite, Dominic Abrams, and Fatima Tresh. "Overlooked Leadership Potential: The Preference for Leadership Potential in Job Candidates Who Are Men vs. Women." *Frontiers in Psychology* 10, no. 755 (2019). https://doi.org/10.3389/fpsyg.2019.00755.

Pratch, Leslie, and Jordan Jacobowitz. "Gender, Motivation, and Coping in the Evaluation of Leadership Effectiveness." *Consulting Psychology Journal: Practice and Research* 48, no. 4 (1996): 203–220. https://doi.org/10.1037/1061-4087.48.4.203.

Prudential. *Pulse of the American Worker Survey: Is This Working?* 2020. https://news .prudential.com/presskits/pulse-american-worker-survey-is-this-working.htm.

PwC. "Putting Purpose to Work: A Study of Purpose in the Workplace." June 2016. https://www.pwc.com/us/en/about-us/corporate-responsibility/assets/pwc-putting -purpose-to-work-purpose-survey-report.pdf.

Quadlin, Natasha. "The Mark of a Woman's Record: Gender and Academic Performance in Hiring." *American Sociological Review* 83, no. 2 (2018): 331–360. https:// doi.org/10.1177/0003122418762291.

Ray, Rebecca, and Beatrice Gretch-Cumbo. "Tactics to Advance Women in the Leadership Pipeline." Conference Board, 2021. https://www.conference-Board.org/blog /human-capital/Women-Leadership-Advancement-Tactics.

Reardon, Kathleen K. "Courage as a Skill." *Harvard Business Review*, January 2007. https://hbr.org/2007/01/courage-as-a-skill.

Reuters. "Uber's Revenue Hits $6.5 Billion in 2016, Still Has Large Loss." April 14, 2017. https://www.reuters.com/article/us-uber-tech-results/ubers-revenue-hits-6-5-billion -in-2016-still-has-large-loss-idUSKBN17G1IB.

Riddle, Douglas. "Your High-Potential Program Could Ruin Your Business." *Harvard Business Review*, July 17, 2012. https://hbr.org/2012/07/your-high-potential-program.

Ryan, Michelle K., and S. Alexander Haslam. "The Glass Cliff: Exploring the Dynamics Surrounding the Appointment of Women to Precarious Leadership Positions." *Academy of Management Review* 32, no. 2 (2007): 549–572. http://www.jstor.org /stable/20159315.

Sandberg, Sheryl. *Lean In: Women, Work, and the Will to Lead*. New York: Knopf, 2013.

Scarborough, William. "What the Data Says about Women in Management between 1980 and 2010." *Harvard Business Review*, February 23, 2018. https://hbr.org/2018 /02/what-the-data-says-about-women-in-management-between-1980-and-2010 ?registration=success.

Schein, Edgar. *Organizational Culture and Leadership*. San Francisco: Jossey-Bass, 2010.

Schulz, Dorothy. "Why Are America's Women Police Chiefs Resigning?" *Crime Report*, August 13, 2020. https://thecrimereport.org/2020/08/13/why-are-americas -women-police-chiefs-resigning/.

Schwartz, Tony. "What Women Know about Leadership That Men Don't." *Harvard Business Review*, October 30, 2012. https://hbr.org/2012/10/what-women-know-that -men-dont.

Searby, Linda J., Julia Ballenger, and Jenny Tripses. "Climbing the Ladder, Holding the Ladder: The Mentoring Experiences of Higher Education Female Leaders." *Advancing Women in Leadership* 35 (2015): 98–107.

Seltzer, Rick. "The Slowly Diversifying Presidency." *Inside Higher Education*, June 20, 2017. https://www.insidehighered.com/news/2017/06/20/college-presidents-diversi fying-slowly-and-growing-older-study-finds.

Shepherd, Ken. "Marissa Mayer Leaves Yahoo with $260M in Severance Pay and Stock: Report." *Washington Times*, June 13, 2017. https://www.washingtontimes.com /news/2017/jun/13/marissa-mayer-leaves-yahoo-260m-severance-pay-and-/.

Shockley, Kristin M., Winny Shen, Michael M. DeNunzio, Maryana L. Arvan, and Eric A. Knudsen. "Disentangling the Relationship between Gender and Work–Family Conflict: An Integration of Theoretical Perspectives Using Meta-analytic Methods." *Journal of Applied Psychology* 102, no. 12 (2017): 1601–1635. https://doi.org/10.1037 /apl0000246.

Shore, Ted H. "Subtle Gender Bias in the Assessment of Managerial Potential." *Sex Roles* 27 (1992): 499–515.

Spencer, Signe M., E. Susanne Blazek, and J. Evelyn Orr. "Bolstering the Female CEO Pipeline: Equalizing the Playing Field and Igniting Women's Potential as Top-Level Leaders." *Business Horizons* 62, no. 5 (2019): 567–577.

Stallbaumer, Collette, and Marissa King. "Work Friends: What the Research Says about Our Ties with Colleagues." *Perspectives* (Microsoft Worklab), n.d. https://www .microsoft.com/en-us/worklab/work-friends.

Stevenson, Jane, and Dan Kaplan. "Women C-Suite Ranks Nudge Up—a Tad." Korn Ferry, 2019. https://www.kornferry.com/insights/articles/women-in-leadership-2019 -statistics.

Stevenson, Jane Edison, and Evelyn Orr. "We Interviewed 57 Female CEOs to Find Out How More Women Can Get to the Top." *Harvard Business Review*, November 8, 2017. https://hbr.org/2017/11/we-interviewed-57-female-ceos-to-find-out-how-more -women-can-get-to-the-top.

Stewart, James B. "A CEO's Support System, aka Husband." *New York Times*, November 4, 2011. https://www.nytimes.com/2011/11/05/business/a-ceos-support-system -a-k-a-husband.html.

Stillman, Jessica. "Michelle Obama Just Said 'Lean In' Doesn't Work. Here's the Study That Proves She's Right." *Inc.*, December 7, 2018. https://www.inc.com/jes sica-stillman/michelle-obama-is-really-not-a-fan-of-sheryl-sandbergs-lean-in.html.

Stone, Pamela, and Meg Lovejoy. "Fast-Track Women and the 'Choice' to Stay Home." *Annals of the American Academy of Political and Social Science* 596, no. 1 (2004): 62–83. doi:10.1177/0002716204268552.

Tannen, Deborah. *Talking 9 to 5*. New York: Harper Collins, 1994.

Taub, Amanda. "Why Are Nations Led by Women Doing Better?" *New York Times*, May 16, 2020.

Tinsley, Catherine H., and Kate Purmal. "Research: Board Experience Is Helping More Women Get CEO Jobs." *Harvard Business Review*, July 29, 2019. https://hbr.org /2019/07/research-Board-experience-is-helping-more-women-get-ceo-jobs.

Tolar, Mary Hale. "Mentoring Experiences of High-Achieving Women." *Advances in Developing Human Resources* 14, no. 2 (2012): 172–187. https://doi.org/10.1177 /1523422312436415.

Tulshyan, Ruchika, and Jodi-Ann Burey. "Stop Telling Women They Have Imposter Syndrome." *Harvard Business Review*, February 11, 2021. https://hbr.org/2021/02 /stop-telling-women-they-have-imposter-syndrome.

Turner Kelly, Bridget. "Though More Women Are on College Campuses, Climbing the Professor Ladder Remains a Challenge." Brookings Institution, March 29, 2019. https://www.brookings.edu/blog/brown-center-chalkBoard/2019/03/29/though -more-women-are-on-college-campuses-climbing-the-professor-ladder-remainsa challenge/#:~:text=Women%20made%20up%2031%20percent,has%20tripled%20 during%20this%20period.

Vanderkam, Laura. *I Know How She Does It: How Successful Women Make the Most of Their Time*. New York: Portfolio, 2017.

Vassallo, Trae, Ellen Levy, Michele Madansky, Hillary Mickell, Bennett Porter, and Monica Leas. "Elephant in the Valley." Survey, n.d. https://www.elephantintheval ley.com/.

Wang, Zhen, Chaoping Li, and Xupei Li. "Resilience, Leadership, and Work Engagement: The Mediating Role of Positive Affect." *Social Indicators Research* 132 (2017): 699–708. https://doi.org/10.1007/s11205-016-1306-5.

Warner, Judith, and Danielle Corley. "The Women's Leadership Gap." Center for American Progress, November 20, 2018. https://www.americanprogress.org/issues /women/reports/2018/11/20/461273/womens-leadership-gap-2/.

Washington, Zuhairah, and Laura Morgan Roberts. "Women of Color Get Less Support at Work: Here's How Managers Can Change That." *Harvard Business Review*, March 4, 2019. https://hbr.org/2019/03/women-of-color-get-less-support-at -work-heres-how-managers-can-change-that.

Weisul, Kimberly. "How Playing the Long Game Made Elizabeth Holmes a Billionaire." *Inc.*, October 2015. https://www.inc.com/magazine/201510/kimberly-weisul /the-longest-game.html.

Williams, Zoe. "*Lean In: Women, Work, and the Will to Lead* by Sheryl Sandberg— Review." *Guardian*, March 13, 2013. https://www.theguardian.com/books/2013 /mar/13/lean-in-sheryl-sandberg-review.

Wing Sue, Derald. "Microaggression: More Than Just Race." N.d. https://www.uua .org/sites/live-new.uua.org/files/microaggressions_by_derald_wing_sue_ph.d._.pdf.

Withisuphakorn, Pradit, and Pornsit Jiraporn. "CEO Age and CEO Gender: Are Female CEOs Older Than Their Male Counterparts?" *Finance Research Letters* 22 (2017): 129–135.

Wittenberg-Cox, Avivah. "If You Can't Find a Spouse Who Supports Your Career, Stay Single." *Harvard Business Review*, October 24, 2017. https://hbr.org/2017/10 /if-you-cant-find-a-spouse-who-supports-your-career-stay-single.

World Economic Forum. "Three Leaders on Creating a Pipeline for Female Talent in Business." March 2020. https://www.weforum.org/agenda/2020/03/3-women-business -leaders-gender-parity-workplace.

Yildirmaz, Ahu, Christopher Ryan, and Jeff Nezaj. *2019 State of the Workforce Report*. Roseland, NJ: ADP Research Institute, 2019. https://www.adpri.org/assets /2019-state-of-the-workforce-report/.

Zarrella, Katharine K. "The Most Powerful Women in Business Wear Power Dresses, Not Suits." *Wall Street Journal*, August 29, 2019. https://www.wsj.com/articles/the -most-powerful-women-in-business-wear-dresses-not-suits-11567106879.

Zenger, Jack, and Joseph Folkman. "Research: Women Score Higher Than Men in Most Leadership Skills." *Harvard Business Review*, June 25, 2018. https://hbr.org /2019/06/research-women-score-higher-than-men-in-most-leadership-skills ?registration=success.

Zweigenhaft, Richard. *The New CEOs*. New York: Rowman & Littlefield, 2011.

Index